Nursing at the Horton -

The Way It Was –

When Care to the Local People Really Mattered

By Dawn Griffis

01869 811746.

1956 to 1965

Nursing Plus

Published by Lulu 2007

Copyright © Dawn Griffis 2007

ISBN 978-84753-865-9

Front cover pictures :
Top: *Horton old entrance, 1950's*
Middle: *1961 Graduation and prize winners group*
Bottom: *Mary Horton*

Title Page:
Old entrance to the Horton General Hospital 1950's

Dedication page:
Student Nurses:
L to R: U/K, Dorothy Hart, Dawn Alsford, Jeanette Boyce

Dedicated to all the SRNs that trained at the Horton General Hospital, Banbury, Oxon.

Preface

As someone who has worked in the NHS myself since 1977, having qualified as a State Registered Nurse (SRN) in 1979, how often have I heard a nurse comment, that their life and working experiences would one day be put in a book. I am delighted to have the pleasure of meeting Dawn Griffis who has done exactly that, remembering her happy days at the Horton General Hospital, some 44 years ago! The fact that Dawn has dedicated her book to all the State Registered Nurses, who trained at the Horton General Hospital, is a reflection of the camaraderie in which Nursing was undertaken, in a much loved local general hospital. I believe there will be many NHS staff, both past and present, who will give a wry smile in recognition of many of the stories and experiences encountered by Dawn, and equally, many of us will reflect on some of the difficult working experiences, encountered by Dawn, before leaving for the USA in 1965. One cannot fail to be unimpressed by Dawn's adaptability of life in the States, and her efforts to carry on with her Nursing career. For my part, as the current Executive Director of the Horton General Hospital, I am delighted Dawn had returned to see "her" Hospital, and to hear how positive she was about some of the environmental changes, but no less determined than most of the local population, as to what the future holds for the Horton General Hospital in an ever changing NHS.

Mike Fleming,
Executive Director,
Horton General Hospital
2007

Table of Contents

Profile		6
Acknowledgements		7
Chapter 1:	Savernake Hospital	9
Chapter 2:	Horton General Hospital- Pre-nursing student days	18
Chapter 3:	Nurses Training	24
Chapter 4:	Goodbye to Gramp	31
Chapter 5:	Early Student Years	35
Pictures		60-79
Chapter 6:	Later Student Years	80
Chapter 7:	Life Changes and Mike	101
Chapter 8:	Between Years	110
Chapter 9:	Goodbye to England	121
Chapter 10:	Horton 44 years Later	124

Profile

Dawn Griffis, nee' Alsford

I was born and raised in Aynhoe, six miles south of Banbury, and just across the border in Northamptonshire.

My nurses training started in March 1956, at Savernake Hospital in Marlborough, Wiltshire. Early in 1957, I transferred to the Horton General Hospital in Banbury, to complete my training.

Shortly afterwards, in 1961, I did a post graduate course in operating theatre nursing.

I married Mike, an American Airman, in 1962 and started a family. We have two daughters and six grandchildren. In 1965, Mike had to return to America, and naturally, I went with him

After 50 years of nursing, where almost forty years of it was spent in many regions of the USA, I returned to England to work. However, because of my age, I was forced to retire in 2006; much earlier than I had planned. This enabled me to finish the two books I started many years ago: 'Aynhoe Village Life - The Way it Was - Then, Before and Beyond', and this one.

I have started writing a third book, 'Living and Nursing in America – The Way it Was – The Good - The Bad and The Ugly', anticipating that it will be published next year.

Currently, 2007, we are enjoying living back in Aynhoe.

Acknowledgements

I would like to say thank you to the following people, for their contributions in bringing this book to fruition.

For photographs and or forms/documents contributed to use:

Vera White nee' Clifton

Christine Lunn nee' Bolton

Alison Bushrod nee' White, who also gave me names and telephone numbers for people to contact.

The Horton Archives through Yolanda Jacobs, Executive assistant to Mike Fleming the Executive Director of the Horton Hospital.

In addition, the time given to me by Yolanda, to tour and explain the changes that have taken place at the Horton for the final chapter, was invaluable. To Mike Fleming for meeting with me, and giving me free access to the Horton, and the use of Yolanda's time; and most especially for writing the preface to the book.

To Ian Huckin, for his time proof reading and editing the book; and continuing to answer all my computer questions in putting the book together.

To my husband Mike Griffis for his support and encouragement during this time, also for driving me wherever I have needed to go; because I am too afraid to drive in England, in light of the crazy drivers I see now see on the roads!

Finally, to the Horton General Hospital, for giving me and many others the excellent nurses training that we received, and teaching us that the patients come first, second and last. Everything else had to fit in-between.

Chapter 1

Savernake Hospital

On 19th March 1956 I started at Savernake Hospital as a pre-nursing student. It was a 78-bed hospital, part of the Oxford Hospital District. It was in a beautiful garden setting on the edge of the Savernake Forest. There was a women's medical / surgical ward, and the same for the men. There was also a small orthopaedic ward for both sexes, which was separated up.

Savernake Hospital 1956

The children's ward was away from the other wards; three of its walls had floor to ceiling windows; creating an unusual sensation when they were practicing breaking the sound barrier, as they did on a daily basis in 1956. It made the entire ward shudder. Off of the children's ward were 4 rooms for the private paying patients.

The children's ward staff staffed them. There was a small emergency room, an area for outpatient visits, and, of course, an operating theatre.

Behind the hospital was the Nurses Home, where all the nursing staff lived. The ground floor had a living room for the Student and Staff Nurses, and a smaller one for the Sisters. They could come into ours but we couldn't go into theirs. The ground floor also had the staff dining room, a small staff kitchen, and the Sisters and Staff Nurses bedrooms. The second floor had Matron's rooms. Hers was a bedroom and living room, (she is a nurse, and her position is that of the head of the nurses and the head of the hospital). The other rooms on that floor, were for some of the Staff Nurses and Student Nurses. The top floor had the bedrooms for the maids that worked throughout the hospital.

Most of the maids there were women who, in the first part of the century, had been inappropriately put into mental hospitals by their families, because they had had illegitimate babies, and they had wanted to hide them away. Or by families that did not want, or could not afford, to bring them up. The current idea was to rehabilitate them, to survive in the world, earn their own living, and to learn to manage their money. This was part of Matrons responsibility. There was a time frame to accomplish this. Some of them got jobs at the hospital on completion, and stayed on in their same jobs. Most of them were pretty basic and loyal people with limited education, but all very hard working and so appreciative of any help that was given them.

We were all given uniforms. The pre-nursing students had blue and white-striped dresses, with the starched white aprons that buttoned at the shoulders, and white starched cap. We had to supply our own black stockings and black shoes. We were not allowed to wear make-up or jewellery. The only exception was, that married women could wear their wedding rings. We had to wear watches that pinned to our apron bibs.

Back L-R Chris Tomlinson, Maureen ? Front L-R Dawn Alsford,, Sylvia ?

The regular Student Nurses' uniform dresses, were solid medium blue, and their aprons pinned on the front below their shoulders. This was the same for the Staff Nurses and Sisters. The Staff Nurses dresses were royal blue, and the Sister's navy blue. Both the Sisters and Staff Nurses' sleeves were to the wrist, with very stiffly starched cuffs that could be taken off, enabling them to roll their sleeves up to work. They would put a frilly white gauze cover over the roll up, to make it look neat. All our caps were the same, except Matron's. Hers was made of lace but stiffly starched. She wore a tailored navy blue dress without an apron. Her name was Miss Blackwell but addressed by all as 'Matron'.

Matrons, in English hospitals in those days, were all powerful. As a student, one would never presume to speak to her, unless first spoken to. If you needed to see her, an appointment was made giving the reason for the meeting. Not that it was necessarily granted. We would never presume to look Matron straight in the eye, but rather kept your eye at about the base of her neck. You never answered any question from her with just a 'yes' or 'no' it always had to be: "Yes Matron", and never volunteer any more conversation than she asked for. Matron did rounds on the wards daily.

Everything had better be spick and span for those, with not a wrinkle in sight. The physicians had to behave the same way to her, except it was only the students that couldn't look her in the eye.

The response, in conversation between the students and the Staff Nurses and Sisters, was the same except calling them just "Staff" or "Sister" was fine. On duty we had to address each other as Nurse followed by their surname. The patients had to address us the same way. There was no such thing as first names, Miss or Mrs. Our mail had to come to us addressed accordingly. During the period I was in training, no matter which hospital it was at, this protocol was maintained.

Nurses Home Savernake Hospital

I was assigned to the children's ward. The Sister's name was Faust. She was German, and a real taskmaster by nature. At the time I thought she was very old, but considering the amount of grey in her hair, she was probably around fifty. She had a very upright posture, and never smiled, except to just one of the students that she seemed to like. I never even saw her smile at any of the patients. When she walked into the ward all was silent. In a children's ward that is usually unheard of. She had a deep voice, and everything she said was as an order, without any please or thank you.

Student Nurses, especially pre-nursing students, did a lot of cleaning. You cleaned clean stuff! Every day we had to take all of the children's clothes out of the drawer's, scrub the drawer's, shake the clothes then refold them, so there were no detectable strings or openings. The large folds had to be to the front of the drawer, the small ones to the side. You could not try skipping a step, as she could always tell. The other daily job we had, was to clean the linen cupboard. This was a one-person job, except you could ask for help refolding the sheets. Again, all the linen had to be taken off the shelves, shaken, refolded, and put back on newly scrubbed shelves. The large folds to the front the small folds on the right, and the selve edges on the left. Each piece of linen had to be stacked in such a way, that when a yardstick was placed against the front and right sides, there was none sticking out. If there was then her little finger came into action: She would hook her little finger, in the bottom piece of the stack, and pull. All would fall onto the floor and she would say: "Now; *do* it again". In a voice with a tone, as if she was a not very nice person training a dog.

That was the tone she used when she told me to do just about anything, including going to lunch or going off duty. I remember one time we had a really nice patient, in one of the private rooms, who had been in a very bad car accident. She had heard Sister Faust talk to me this way for about a week, when she called me into her room. She asked me why I put up with her talking to me like that. I told her it was just her way; maybe they talk that way where she comes from.

After that, the patient used to have me come into her room, on the pretence of wanting me to do something for her. Instead she just wanted to give me a break. Sister never entered her room without knocking, so it gave time for me to be doing something when she came in, that we had pre-planned. She would always tell me to get out and go back to work. The patient would say: "No. Not until I am finished with her." I always found patients in England to be very protective of their nurses. It is a very special relationship we have with them, and even the difficult ones were very special.

Besides the cleaning that we did constantly, we also learned to make the different kinds of beds. Believe it or not, there are multiple ways and types of beds to make, besides the traditional ones with the hospital corners. From ones with the patients still in them, to beds for when they are coming back from the operating theatre, to orthopaedic beds, and ones for patients with splints or in traction.

It was not only Matron that did rounds, but the physicians did also. When this occurred, the bed covers over the patient, had to have the least amount of wrinkles possible. For all patients that were confined to bed, we were taught always to pull up on the covers over their feet, to prevent foot drop. This can easily occur from pulling bed covers over their feet too tightly. I still yank on the covers over their feet, when I pass a bed with a patient in it.

We were expected to entertain the children during the day, after we had bathed and fed them all. There were occasionally times when we had to help hold a child, while a treatment was being given to them. We also helped transport patients back and forth to the operating theatre, or to outpatient clinics if the doctor wanted to see them there.

Between our ward and the operating room, there was a ninety-degree angle bend in the passageway. Back in those days, patients weren't strapped onto the trolleys. This one day a patient was being transported to the theatre. He had had his pre-op medication, so he was asleep. The theatre staff had called, and said to get him down there fast. So they did! The only thing was that they took the corner too fast! They went round the bend and the patient didn't! They got him back on the trolley, and while he was in surgery, they x-rayed his whole body, found nothing broken, and carried on with the surgery. After surgery the patient said: "Well, that was uneventful." He had no ill effects or memory of it. The Matron did tell him what happened. He just passed it off that he didn't even have a bruise.

Generally speaking, all we did was clean; most especially the utility room, where the bedpans were kept. This was usually our first job each morning. They used to tell us; if we did not understand the importance of cleaning, and that no job is a small or insignificant job, then we won't understand the importance of the more complex and involved jobs. It was the cleaning that prevented wound infection, and cross contamination. I must admit I never saw a wound infection, which was hospital induced, in the 6 plus years I nursed in England.

We had a very sick 2 year old come in. His parents had apparently never fed him anything but milk. About a week before, he had stepped on a rusty nail that had broken the skin on his foot. They hadn't done anything about it; neither had he received any tetanus injections. He was admitted into isolation in one of the private rooms. Mostly to keep it quiet for him, and in semi darkness. He was to have no stimulus.

It was necessary to have someone sitting with him 24 hours a day, to monitor his jaw, so that he did not bite his tongue when he went into the seizure type rigours. The rigours had to be counted and the duration noted. Obviously I was not knowledgeable enough on the disease at that time, to know what they were using for treatments. I think the reason they used me as the nurse, to be with him during the daytime, was because of the experience I had had with the boys at the hospital, and dealing with their seizures. He went into some awful rigours, with his teeth and jaw locked so tightly, that I could understand why the common name for it is lockjaw.

At first they really didn't think he had much chance of surviving. I asked them what I could do, to make it more hopeful for him. They said to just keep talking to him, very gently and soothingly, and to touch him gently so he was aware of someone being there. The human contact, and not feeling alone, is very important during this stage in any illness. I really wasn't sure how much good I was doing, but he steadily improved to the point where he could go out into the main ward. Our job then was to feed him up to gain his strength and increase his activity to strengthen his muscles.

Before long he was standing at the end of his cot (crib), with his arms out-stretched, waiting for me to walk past him. If I was close enough, then he would grab me around my neck and pull me towards him. He never did this to anyone else. Sister said it was because of the hours I spent with him, talking to him and comforting him, that he was aware, probably only subconsciously, that I am different from the others to him. From that time on, she did seem to treat me a little differently. Maybe I had finally done something right in her eyes.

We worked long hours; anywhere from 8 to 12 hours a day, with 1 day off a week. Sometimes we got off at 6 pm the day before our day off, instead of 8:30pm. Then it seemed like it was a longer break. For this we got room and board, and the aforementioned uniforms. That included a navy blue, red lined woollen cape, to wear over our uniforms when we were outdoors. In addition, we were paid a pound a week, to allow us to purchase any personal needs we had. All student nurses in England got a stipend. They did, of course, take deductions out for National Insurance and taxes. We just ended up with a pound, which to us, at that time, was all that mattered.

The dining room in the nurses' home, was very gracious. It was carpeted, and there were 3 dining room tables. Two of the tables were large enough for twelve people. The third was smaller, large enough for six, which was used mostly for people who were off duty, and not confined to eating at the set times. The tables were highly polished with a dark finish, and the chairs were of a classic design. The large table, by the windows, was for Matron (at the head), the sisters and staff nurses. The other table was for the student and pre-student nurses. The tables were laid as if in a very high-class restaurant. With light blue place mats, that covered the cork mats, to protect the finish from hot plates. The places were set, with the multiple cutlery's, according to the meal being served, with the main plate on the table to receive the other plates when we were served. We only had water to drink with the meal. Prior to starting the meal, we all had to be there on time. No tardiness was permitted. We had to stand behind our chairs until Matron had said grace. She then instructed us to be seated. The meal was served to us in order of status, Matron first, sisters next and so on. Vegetables were served in covered silver bowls in the centre of the tables. When the lids were lifted off, the steam rose letting off enticing smells. The meat entrée was served to us individually. When all were served at your table, we could help ourselves to the vegetables. When finished the same routine took place with the dessert. On completion of the dessert, we were allowed to go to the kitchen, just off the dining room, and help ourselves to drink, after we had gone besides Matron's chair, and asked for permission to leave.

This is the only hospital I have ever worked in, that I can honestly say the food was beyond anyone's wildest dreams; it was fabulous. Besides the dining room atmosphere, the presentation just added to the incredible flavour. On the cooks day off Matron did the cooking, I think she must have liked to cook, because it wasn't a requirement for her to do it. Her cooking was definitely on par with the cooks. I have eaten in hospitals for the past 50 years, and I am sorry to say never experienced such food ever again. The patients got the same food as we did, and they never complained either.

From very early on, when I decided I wanted to be a nurse, I was fascinated with the thought of working in the operating theatre. It is generally accepted that you don't get that experience, until about your third year of training. I couldn't wait that long. I noticed from my bedroom window, that there was a window on the slant in the roof, over where the theatre was located. There was also a metal ladder attached to the wall, behind the back of the building to the roof. When I heard one night that there was emergency surgery being performed, I sneaked out of the nurse's home, and up on the roof I went. It was even better than it first appeared, for there was a low wall on either side of the window, giving me a perfect seat to sit and watch the surgery going on below. The window was in a perfect spot for seeing right over the operating table. From that time on, whenever night time surgery was happening, I was there. Some of the other students found out what I was doing, and kept begging me to let them come as well. Finally, one night, I said ok, and about four of us went out. We had no sooner got comfortable, and were enjoying what we were watching, when lights were flashed on us and we were told to come down.

By the time we had scrambled down, and were standing in a line in front of night sister and a local policeman, our pyjama pant legs were creeping down below our coats. They asked what we were doing, and I told them we were watching the surgery going on in the theatre. They asked whose idea it was. Of course I had to say it was mine. The others were told to leave and not to do it again. I was told I was going to be reported to Matron and to expect to be called to her office in the morning. This turned out to be the first of many trips I made, to different Matrons offices over the next several years. I didn't know it, but there had been a prowler sighted around the hospital, and that was why they spotted us, because they were watching for activity outside.

The next morning I was summoned to Matrons office, as predicted.

She asked me why I was up on the roof, and how long had I been doing it. I told her I had been doing since shortly after I had started there, and it was because I wanted to be a theatre nurse, and didn't want to wait so long before I saw any surgeries. She told me about the prowler, and that it wasn't safe for young girls to be out after dark, especially alone in as remote an area as we were. That in the future, if it wasn't too late, if there was emergency surgery going on, and if it was all right with the surgeon, then I could go into the theatre and watch. She probably thought it better in there, than for me to be up on a roof. I did get to go in to watch the surgeries. The view was very inadequate, compared to the view from the roof, but it was better than nothing.

About the end of October, I started to get a swelling in my right wrist. I thought I had probably hurt it lifting one of the adult patients. Then one day I took a large glass bottle from off a shelf, and it slipped through my hand as if there was nothing there to hold it. I went to get a brush and dustpan to clean it up, and I couldn't lift anything with my right hand. The staff nurse on duty sent me to the ER to have it checked. Luckily it was the day the orthopaedic specialist was there from Oxford, so he examined it. He told me what was wrong, said I had to be put in a cast to my elbow for 6 weeks to rest it, and to not get my fingers wet. When I got back to the ward, the staff asked me what he had said was wrong with it. I told her what I thought he said. I told her it sounded like I had; "an attack of tired itis". She laughed and said she would find out what it was. It was tenosynovitis in the wrist. I was limited to working with just one hand, which is not an easy task in nursing. It was only a couple of weeks and then my left wrist was in the same, if not a worse situation, than my right and with a cast on both arms. It rapidly became apparent, that I was not going to be able to rest and heal the wrists if I kept working. I was sent home with instructions, as much as anything for my mother, that I had to rest until the casts came off, and then I was going to need therapy to re-strengthen them. Mum was not happy having me home, and not being able to help around the house.

It took longer to heal than was expected, and I was able to receive my therapy up at the hospital, from one of their physiotherapists. During this time I received a letter from Matron, saying that she wanted to meet with my father and me. Dad and I went as soon as he was able to get away. Matron said she had talked to the orthopaedic surgeon, and he thought it very unlikely my wrists would ever be strong enough to continue nursing. She thought it better for me to plan on doing some other kind of work. I told her I was going to be a nurse, no matter what it took. She said she hoped I would, but that I needed to take my belongings home with me, because she thought it would be a very long time before that would happen.

I was devastated and angry. Dad helped me pack and get my belongings home. He said that if I worked hard with the therapists, on strengthening my wrists, then at least I would know I had really tried even if it didn't happen. After a lot of hard work on all our parts, by the middle of January we thought my wrists were strong enough to try again. I was told if they started to show signs of a problem, just to wrap them in ace bandage at least overnight, to give them a rest and some support. To this day I still have to do that on occasions.

Chapter 2

Horton General Hospital –pre nursing student days

It was just under a year after I had first been accepted at Savernake, and I was looking for another hospital to train in. I tried the Radcliffe, only to be told that they had a policy, that the student nurses not live in the town they were going to train in. It was too easy to run home when things got bad. That should have told me what I was in for, but of course, I was so determined that I was not listening to any hidden meaning. I was advised that Banbury had a very good nursing school, and it was part of the Oxford Hospital District. Banbury was also only six miles from Aynhoe.

I applied and sent the needed recommendations. These also included the fact that my wrists were now healed, and if sensible should not obstruct my training. This time I went for my interview on my own. I was accepted, and scheduled to report there in early - February 1957. The Horton, as it is commonly and affectionately known, was a 210-bed hospital, with the nurses home attached to it. Let me say at the offset, the food there was atrocious for all, or at least it seemed it after the Savernake food. They could make good party snacks, and brains or sweetbreads in white sauce, but the rest was awful. The Horton was to be my home, nursing school and workplace for the next 5 plus years.

Anne Johnson (Mousey)

I became very close from the start, with two other pre-nursing students, and we were together until I left in 1962. Anne Johnson, nicknamed Mousey, was just over five feet tall, and Doreen Pickersgill, nicknamed Pickers, was close to five feet eleven. I didn't have a nickname, and I was five feet seven. I am sure the three of us looked comical walking together. We always walked very fast, and very few people could keep up with us. Considering Anne's height, it was quite an accomplishment for her to keep up with us.

The uniforms for the staff, other than the pre-nursing students, were the same as those at Savernake. Ours were a light brown dress, and our apron bibs were the same as the others, ending below our shoulders.

We did not work on the wards, until the last 2-3 months before we started our nurses training proper. At that time we were assigned to the children's ward, and then our uniforms changed to the medium blue of the student nurses.

The pre-nursing education at the Horton, was considerably different from Savernake, in as much we had to work in all departments of the hospital, before going near a ward. The concept was; that there is more to running a hospital than wards and nurses. If we have some understanding of what the other departments were doing, and the importance of their work, it would lead to a better-run hospital. It made perfect sense to me; not that my opinion counted for much in those days.

Because I started a year later at the Horton than the others did, having been at Savernake my first year, I didn't get to work in as many departments as Mousey and Pickers did. My first assignment was the accounting and purchasing department. With my aptitude for maths, I fitted in there very quickly. They seemed disappointed when the time came for me to move on. I did not stay a stranger to them. I frequently stopped by to see them, throughout my ongoing years there.

My next assignment was the hospital supply and distribution centre. True to its name, all supplies, including food, came in through here, and had to be delivered to all areas throughout the hospital. That was my job. This gave my wrists a real workout, but it also taught me how to lift, and it definitely built muscle. It also gave me the opportunity to meet just about everyone who worked there. Of course, that meant many more people knew who I was, and, in the future, it was harder to get away with anything without being recognized!

I did a very short stint in the laboratory when it was still in the basement, before it moved upstairs to a nice bright department. I also filled in occasionally in both medical records and Matron's administrative office. But my last months, before going onto the wards, were in the X-ray department. The staff there really took the time explaining what they did, and allowed me to help with the patients being X-rayed. If there was fluoroscopy being done, the physician would have me stand beside him, so he could explain the workings going on inside the patient. I thought it was all very fascinating. The physician also had me in the office with him, when he was reading the X-rays, so he could point out what was normal versus abnormal. This particular physician had been the one that invented the square or cross markings used on X-ray machines to this day, making it easier to pinpoint the area they are trying to X-ray. They also let me work in the dark room, to learn how to develop the X-rays. They were a great group of people to work with, and I was really very sorry when the time came for me to leave to go onto the wards.

During this period there was something that happened to me, which eventually had a considerable effect on me. A patient came into the female medical ward, with a very bad case of diarrhoea. By the time they had a diagnosis of full-blown dysentery, two of the nurses had come down with it too. One had her room in the same corridor as mine. We were all told we would be alright, because they were in isolation, and had commodes in their rooms to use, so as to not contaminate the two toilets in our section.

About a week later, I started having diarrhoea very badly, but did not think it was anything to worry about, because "we were safe" from catching it. When I woke in the night, with cramps so bad I thought I would die, all I was passing was blood, I knew this was more than it should be. When Pickers came by my room, to see why I wasn't at breakfast, she could see how ill I was, and went and got Molly, our nickname for the home sister.

After much investigation, they found out that the senior staff nurse in my corridor had been using the same toilet at night time, that I had used regularly. That's where I caught it. She had won all the medals during her training, for her class work and exam results, but when it came to functioning on the wards, and with patients she was totally incompetent. Also her techniques left much to be desired. She didn't believe she would pass it on just by using the toilet! I guess it is thanks to her, that I have little respect for people with all kinds of book-learning capabilities, and prizes for passing an exam etc. They have to prove themselves, and their real capabilities, in functioning in the real world of patients, before they gain my recognition or respect.

It took over a week of just sips of water, medication and rest, before I could even have a slice of toast to eat. Molly was so sweet to me, she told me that it wasn't my fault I had it so bad. There was no reason for me to suspect I had it, but by the time I realized something was really wrong, it had a very strong hold on me. I didn't contaminate anyone else because I was working in accounting at the time, and as it happened, the only bathroom I used was the one in our corridor.

The first meal of toast I had, tasted so good. Molly brought it to me on a tray, with a pretty white lace tray cloth on it, along with a small vase with a fresh flower in it. The cutlery was silver, the delicate floral china was bone china and included tea plate, cup and saucer, sugar bowl and milk jug, all complimented with a silver teapot with very weak tea in it. She explained it needed to be that way, because I would not be able to handle any stimulant. The toast was a light golden brown without any butter on it. She had cut the crust off cut it into tiny thin triangular shapes, arranged on the plate in a design to make it look very appealing. She advised me to stay in bed, and to eat and drink it very slowly. If I were able to eat this, without setting off another cycle of diarrhoea and cramping, she would be able to gradually increase my diet. In my lifetime I have eaten many meals - some quite exotic - but none that tasted as good as that meal did, and so beautifully presented. I think she really felt sorry for me and all I went through, and she was trying very hard to make it up to me. I appreciated enormously. To be able to work, I needed 3 negative stools. They were not forthcoming, so after 2 weeks I was sent home to recuperate. It was another 4 weeks before I had 2 negative stools. By then they said that was good enough and I could come back.

Nurses room in the Nurses Home

The last of my pre nursing student days, was spent on the children's ward known as, Holbech, prior to going into preliminary school. This was educational, and a valuable step prior to starting our training proper. Mousey, Pickers and I, all started at the same time on the ward in December. Mousey and Pickers were going to start their prelims in January, because of how their birthdays fell. I wasn't going to start until March, because
I wasn't going to be 18 until February. We hated it that we were going to be separated this way, even though we were still classified as being in the same school year.

Sister Stewart was less than 5 feet tall, and was an excellent nurse and teacher, as was the senior Staff Nurse Margaret Mac Cue and the junior staff nurse Vera Clifton. They ran Holbech. The ward was in the oldest part of the hospital, so the windows were high like those in Aynhoe School. As you entered the main door, there was a private room to the left for an adult, if the other private rooms in the rest of the hospital were full. It was rarely used. There was another door into the main ward, to Sister's office in the left-hand corner, and the kitchen was off the right hand side. Half way down this wall was a door to the treatment medication room. There was a large table that ran through the centre of the ward for eating at, and/or playing games, so there were chairs all around it. Beds were on opposite walls running lengthwise down the ward. There was a place at the end of the there was a large door to the back section. On either side were private rooms for children that needed isolation. This led into a hall with the utility room, supply room, and linen cupboard going off the left side. The right side led to another ward that had partitions in the room, but had either six cots or beds in it. There were two additional private rooms off of there, again for isolation if needed. It was in this back room, where it was quieter and more private, that the babies with hydrocephalus and spina bifida were cared for. There was a ruling that no hospital would care for more than two babies with these conditions at a time. The reason for this was; that it was deemed too stressful for the nurses. It was rare that we had none but occasionally we would only have one.

The spina bifida babies we had were usually the very severe ones, where their whole spinal cord was in a ball at the base of their spine. It looked like a black lump about a size of a 3-inch ball. These babies rarely lived more than a few weeks. With hydrocephalus babies the simplest way to explain this is; that they have fluid on the brain. These babies could live much longer but rarely past a year.

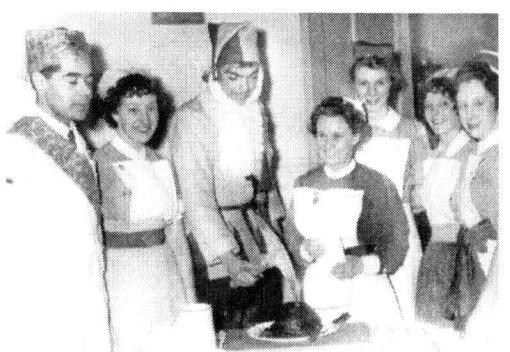

Holbech Ward Xmas 1957 L-R John Caras-Altus, Vera White, Dr Pickering, Sister Stewart, Margaret Hammer, Jean Paxton, Cynthia Holowell

Nowadays they can put shunts in; to drain and keep the fluid drained off, but back in the 50's we did not have that option.

We had one baby with hydrocephalus named Jane who lived to be well over a year old. She ended up with the questionable distinction of developing the largest head on record. It took two people to hold her head and to turn her, which we did every hour night and day. This was to try to prevent bedsores on the side of her head. But even with that, she developed gangrenous sores on both sides of her head. There was no way of telling if she was in pain. She had a healthy appetite and drank her formula well. Her face was normal size, and very pretty, with Dresden like complexion. Her head was enlarged from her eyebrows to the nape of her neck. It was about a foot thick across her head, and at least eighteen inches long from the front to the base at the back of her neck. It was very heavy, so to turn her, one had to hold and steady her head, and the other person had to hold and steady her body, and then turn her simultaneously. Otherwise the weight of her head would have snapped her neck and killed her.

I have to admit that, during the many hours I would sit and feed her, wondering if she was suffering, I could not imagine that she wasn't. I would think how easy it would be to cover her nose and mouth and let her rest. Her parents could no longer stand to visit her. It was just we nurses who loved and cared for her, and we could not escape the fact that we felt it was cruel keeping her alive. We would talk about her amongst ourselves. We all felt the same way, but knew we couldn't do anything about it. Thankfully she died at about 15 months old. I think it was a good thing we were not allowed to take care of more than two at a time. It still brings tears to my eyes to think of her.

On Holbech we still had all the cleaning to do, but Sister made sure we had more to do than just clean. I was to find out she was the exception to the rule.

Chapter 3

Nurses Training

Preliminary school time, was the formal start of nurses training in the late 1950's and early 60's in England. Mine started in mid March. There was to be only four of us in the class. I was the only one that had done any pre-nursing student time, so the others were pretty green.

Christine Bolton came from Banbury. There didn't seem to be a problem, about living and training in the same town, any longer,. Dorothy Hart came from the village of Hanwell, just north of Banbury. Chris and Dot were long time friends, and were both 19. Jeanette Boyce was in her 20's and came from Barbados. We all became good friends, but I was closer to Jeanette, mainly because, at first, Chris and Dot were very giggly and seemed very immature to me. Plus, because they lived close to the hospital, they were not required to live in the nurses' home, therefore you do not get to know them as well.

Student Nurses in class

In prelims we were to be in class Monday though Friday, from 8 am to 5pm. I hadn't worked such short hours since the Potato Marketing Board. Dot and Chris had never worked such long hours! This was the only time we were in concentrated classes, until the last six months of our training. At that time they initiated study blocks for the students, but during the bulk of our training, we had to get our lectures in our spare time, or after working on the wards. This entailed working on the wards 60 to 72 hours a week. The last year of our training, they reduced our working hours for all students to 48 then 44. That is just so long as we had our work done. If not, then we were expected to stay until it was finished. Therefore, it is understandable that we appreciated the luxury of having every weekend off, for the first 3 months of training.

Classes in prelim, were designed to give us the basic nursing hygiene of the patients and ourselves, including the care of a patient in isolation. Classes included anatomy and physiology, plus materia medica. The basic nursing skills taught during the 50's and 60's were, what is now considered, back in the dark ages. It was before dip sticks for urine testing, before disposable supplies or equipment, and definitely before pre-packaged or pre-made anything. This meant we had to learn to make it all, from cotton balls to many tail bandages. We even patched the rubber gloves that were to be sterilized for any sterile technique, even for surgeries. If I had a penny for all the gauze 4x4's I have made, I'd be wealthy. Plus how to launder supplies that were re-usable, especially face masks and babies nappies.

Intravenous sets, for giving IV fluids and/or blood, were made up of red rubber tubing, that was joined with a couple of glass connectors. These connectors were placed in the tube, in the hope that, if there was a blockage, it would be right there so you could see why it wasn't running. You could then milk the tubing and get it to run again. In addition there was the glass chamber with the wire mesh trap and drip tube, so you were able to count how fast the fluid or blood was running. The tubing was connected to a straight needle that went into a vein, and the other end had a metal needle like connection, that went into the bottle of either blood or fluid. Any part of these contraptions, could and would forever plug up, or just not run at all. We spent more time working and nursing them along, than with anything else. When the patient was through with the administration of the IV, it did not end with us throwing it away as is done today. That was not an option. We had to clean it all, and then sterilize it ready for the next patient.

We learned the names of all the different tubes, catheters and drains and what they were used on or in the patient, plus what they were used for. Again we were taught the care and maintenance of them, for these were not discarded unless they were worn out. Syringes were glass or metal and again used and re-used after sterilizing, along with the needles for injections. With the needles we would sharpen and re-sharpen the points, until there was nothing but stub ends before they were tossed out. We would test the needles, to see if they needed sharpening, by running our thumbnail up the shaft of the needle. If it hooked on the end, it needed sharpening. I always felt sorry for the patient that had been on the receiving end of that particular needle.

We were also taught how to give the most painless injections possible, especially considering what we had to work with. For an injection to not be felt, it needs to go in very fast. The best way to do it, is to throw it in as if you are throwing a dart. They will not feel a thing. They may feel the actual medicine going in, because some medications have that tendency. We can't have any control over that. I have never had anyone complain about my injections. The response usually, when I tell them it's all done is, "I didn't feel a thing." If the medication is going to hurt I warn them, because they will always imagine it will be worse than it really is. There is a sensation that we have sometimes, that is awful to us but never felt by the patient, and that is if they are very thin then the needle will hit the bone. They don't feel it, but we do, and it is a most unpleasant sensation.

Back in those days we had to learn how to do many kinds of bandaging. Some were fun to be able to accomplish, with the patterns that were supposed to show, so as to demonstrate they were done correctly. If done correctly, they would hold up with the patients' movement. I loved to do the arms and legs with the "V" shaped patterns. I was terrible at the skull bandages. With those, to know you have done it right, you are supposed to be able to remove it from the head and it still remains in the shape of the skull. Mine never did!

The other thing we learned during prelims was how to clean and the importance of it. We cleaned everything, and nothing was left unclean. We were taught it was the only sure way of preventing cross contamination between patients. We even scrubbed and scraped the wheels on beds, carts, trolleys. In fact if it had a wheel it was scraped and scrubbed. Even with a patient in the bed if needs be.

In those days, we were also taught how to do the basic lab tests on urine and stools. This meant boiling the urine in test tubes over a Bunsen burner, and adding the chemicals needed to get the required test done. We also tested stools, most commonly for blood, but on occasions we would have to put it through a sieve, to try to find the head of a tapeworm. The first year out on the wards, we spent many hours in the utility rooms each morning, cleaning bedpans, urinals, testing urine and stools. Now it is so easy, if a dipstick can't do it, then it goes to the labs for the testing.

Theatre Nurse doing laundry 1958 L-R ? Dunkley, Ann Hunt, Vera Clifton, Eileen Heritage

I believe the two most important things that were taught to us, and were on-going throughout our training were - the most dangerous nurse in the world, was the one that did everything by the book. That we were to consider the textbook as guidelines for the basis of nursing and medical knowledge, not the be all and end all; that the human being that fell into the true text book situation, was rare to non-existent. If our minds were locked into that mind set, we would lose, or harm, a lot of patients. I wish the students were taught that today.

The second thing taught was the importance of being observant; that this, along with an open mind, would save a lot of lives. We were taught to start off practicing this as a game. To glance at a person, and then to tell a companion all that you noticed in that glance, from the clothes they were wearing to any physical attributes, from face shape, colour, hair, complexion etc. We used to test each other with this everywhere we went. It does not take very long, and you can become very good at it, to the point you do it without even thinking about it. To this day, all I have to do is think back to where I was on any given day or place, and I can give that information on just about anyone I saw. I can do the same thing with whatever was said too. This can be very disconcerting to some people.

The next step with observation, after we had this off pat, especially as we learned more about diseases and the signs they show, was to now look at people, and figure out what we thought might be wrong with them. Of course, some are very obvious, as in the patients with jaundice, but there are others much more subtle. Such as the Dresden china complexion of a TB patient, or the eggshell complexion of the pernicious anaemia patient, to the dull expressionless overweight appearance of the hypothyroid patient, and the hollowed sunken eye appearance, and sallow complexion of the person with cancer.

We would see these people on the streets and play this game. Because Banbury was small enough in those days, it was not unusual for us to come across these people that we had seen in town and to find out just how accurate we were. This often gave us a funny feeling, as to: "Should we stop them and tell them?" We thought about it, but we never did. The observation skills we learned though, have stood me in good stead throughout my career. My hope is for the betterment of my patients. It definitely goes a long way, to be able to diagnose a patient's illness. That is along with a good history and physical. This is so that tests are only ordered, to confirm ones suspicion as to the diagnosis, rather than to randomly order tests, in the hope of hitting on the right diagnosis. Sadly this is the way it is frequently done nowadays. Maybe this is reason for the rising cost of health care.

Subsequent lectures during our training encompassed the operation of the more complex equipment, or new things as they were developed. The last year of my training, was when we started getting the disposable syringes and IV sets. 'Praise be to the Lord', when those came about. The amount of work they saved was incredible.

The rest of our lectures were mainly from physicians or surgeons, and related to diseases. English nurses are taught the signs and symptoms of a disease, how to diagnose and treat it. This is not the way it is done in the US, where the nurses are only allowed to just give what they call nursing diagnosis; it is still that way even today. The only exception to that, are the Nurse Practitioners. It makes me wonder if the physician's egos are so fragile, or if they are so insecure that they are frightened the nurse will outshine them. The American nurse is never to presume to say it is "so and so." That is the physician's prerogative only. What do they think we are? Morons? Nurses, in the US for example, have to say a patient appears to be dead etc. Come on now dead is dead! Just about anyone can recognize that.

English nurses, in those days, were also taught, and had the total responsibility for; when dressings needed changing, sutures removing, drains shortened and removed. We also decided what diets the patients was given, and when they were to be progressed to normal diets. We also decided when patients were ready for discharge home. We would tell the physician, and he would write the order. A physician would never presume to make any of those aforementioned decisions. And woe betides any physician who even considered touching a wound! Once surgery was over, that was our territory. Physicians were always known as the great contaminators. Even in the operating theatre, the nurses watched the surgeons closely, to make sure they did not contaminate themselves or the operating site.

It was protocol, in those days, for nurses to give up their seat for a physician, to open doors for them, and to address them with respect. In the same instance, in England, the physicians showed respect to the nurse, with regards to how they were addressed and for their knowledge and skills. I never heard a nurse or a physician, ever talk disrespectful about the other. For that matter, neither one deserved any less.

At the end of prelims we took our prelim exam. This was the first of the State required exams to become an SRN. The next set of exams was about a year later, then the finals at the end of three years. Actually it was usually three years and three months later. The finals were in several parts that took all day, over 3 days. They also included half a day of orals that took place later in Oxford. The written exams were in essay format, which test your knowledge, rather than the multiple choices, which in reality only test your guessing power. Each exam covered separate disciplines, e.g. medicine, surgery, ob/gyne, paediatrics. The psychiatry was incorporated into each discipline; because it was their belief a person reacts differently, according to what was wrong with them.

Each exam comprised 5 questions, and it was expected that each question would take a half-hour to complete. We could take each question in whatever order we chose. Spelling and grammar mistakes did not go against you; all they were interested in was the content. At least this way we could remember all the questions asked, allowing us the opportunity to check them out afterwards to see how close we were. I only remember one of my questions on one of the exams. It was; what are the signs and symptoms, and how do you diagnose and treat cancer of the prostate. Include any medications that are used in the treatment. I did fine on the signs and symptoms and the diagnosis, but I was way ahead of the time on treatment, because I operated on him and removed the prostate, and only used medications for pain. In those days they did not operate for cancer of the prostate.

It took six weeks before we got the results of our exams. It was the tradition in Banbury, that the night the results were coming into the post office, the nurses would go down at 2 am. The postal workers would have them all pulled out, waiting for them when they got there. If the envelope was thin, and only had a ½ d stamp on it, the nurse had passed. If it was thick and had more postage on, it meant the nurse had failed. The extra content was the form to submit, to re-take it next time they came around. We were never told our scores. It was just a pass or fail, so if you failed, you had no idea how close you were. The scores are not available to anyone; those are probably the best-kept secrets anywhere. At the completion of prelims, we had to take a week's holiday, prior to going to the Wards we had been assigned to. In fact, they liked us to take a week's holiday every three months when our rotations changed. The belief was; that with the work and the stress we had, it was in everyone's interest to not work any longer than 3 months without a break. We were usually ready for it to.

The training agreement we had with the hospital, was that we would rotate through all the wards and departments, at each level of competence that we had been educated to. This was to enable us to meet the level of education, for a qualified SRN. This had to include 3 months of night duty, at each year's level of training.

The wards included separate male and female medical wards: A-Ward for the men and B-Ward for the women. Male and female surgical/orthopaedic wards: C-Ward for the men and D-Ward for the women. All of these wards had 36 beds in them, plus one private and one amenity room. The private patients paid for all their care. The amenity patient still received their medical care under the national health. They just paid for their room. The Gynaecological and Paediatric Wards had 20 –30 beds, with a single private room attached to each. The Elms - the obstetric ward - was separate from the rest of the hospital, in a former mansion type house. We only rotated through the departments once, and that was in our senior or third year. This included; Emergency Room, Operating Theatre and Out Patient's Department. My first assignment was to be back on paediatrics.

Chapter 4

Goodbye to Gramp

During prelims, I was able to spend every weekend with Gran and Gramp, which we all enjoyed. Right about the same time it became obvious that Gramp was getting a lot weaker, and he did not look well. He wouldn't allow the Doctor to examine him. When Dr McCabe suggested he didn't need to get up so early, but to rest more, he got up half an hour earlier. McCabe thought he had misunderstood so he tried again, then he got up half an hour earlier than that. As he said; he daren't say more: He'll never go to bed.

By this time Gran, Mum and her brothers were getting very worried about him, so they asked me if I would talk to him. They pointed out; "you are his favourite, you are the only one he listens to." I told them I would try, but he is stubborn and he may not listen to me. The decision was, if he wouldn't listen to me, there was nothing else that could be done. Gramp and I were up in the garden just talking; when he said; "So what do they want you to say to me." I was straight with him and told him. I also said; I really wish if you won't let McCabe examine you, at least try to take it a bit easier. Either stay in bed a bit longer or go to bed earlier. He said he knew he was sick, but the only way he knew to beat it, was to not give up. I told him that was fine, but just give his body time to rest. He agreed to stay in bed longer, and go to bed earlier, but he wouldn't see McCabe.

Around the eighth of June I was home and Gramp was much weaker. He sat at the table, and emptied all his money out of his pocket. It was just change. He divided it into two piles, and then took four pennies out of them and asked me to do a favour for him. He wanted me to take each pile of money: One was for me to buy a gift for June, for her birthday on the 19th, and the other pile was to get Gran a really nice bouquet of roses from Mr Taylor, for her birthday on the 25th. The other four pennies he said he was going to keep, so he wouldn't die a pauper. I told him he didn't need to do that. That he would be here for their birthdays. He said: "No I won't" and he needed to know I would do that for him. I said I would. It was 4:30pm and he said he thought he would go up to bed. He was very tired, and asked if I would walk upstairs behind him to steady him. He got his candle and lit it, said goodnight to Gran, and we went upstairs. When he was settled I kissed him goodnight, and went downstairs. He never regained consciousness in the house again.

31

In the morning, when we realized his condition, the family gathered and the decision was to try and care for him ourselves, so he could die at home. They thought that, with my help, they could do it if we all took shifts. I got all the equipment I thought we would need to accomplish this, and worked out the shifts. Dr McCabe was very supportive. I took the evening shift after classes, and then was home over the whole weekend.

By the weekend we noticed some unusual physical changes in him. His hands had been gnarled with deformation from arthritis. Now his hands looked perfectly normal with no signs of any arthritis. When we looked at his knees, they were the same. It was very unusual. He seemed in no discomfort; just very peaceful. By Monday, though he was getting very dehydrated. We were no longer able to get any liquids into him. I called McCabe and asked about starting an IV just for the fluids. He said if he needs an IV, then he needs to be in the hospital. So that is where he went. I told Gran I would be with him, whenever I wasn't in class. Those promises made her feel better.

During the first 24 hours he was there, I had just arrived on the ward and Sister Regan said that our vicar was there to see him. I went to see who it was and saw it was Mr. Banham. I told him that

George Edward Parrish 1877 to 1958 (Gramp)

Gramp wouldn't have anything to do with him when he had a say in it, and he wasn't going to see him now, and for him not to try again. He left. I told Sister Regan he was to never be allowed to see him. She was a Catholic and very upset with me for doing such a thing. So, quick thinking, I said that Gramp was raised a Catholic and that I was going to talk to one of the priests in Banbury. She was fine with that. So off I went to St Johns, explained the situation to the priest, and told him he had been excommunicated when he married Gran. He said they used to do that a lot. It was ok; he would rectify it that day.

The next day, June 18th, Gramp regained consciousness. We had had classes changed for some reason, and were off in the afternoon. We were to go back for a class in the evening. I was able to tell Gramp about Mr. Banham and the Catholic priest, and what I had done. He told me I had done the right thing. Just before five, I told him I was going to have to go back to class, but I would be back as soon as we were through. He asked me what the time was, and I told him almost five. He said "All right my duck, goodnight, god bless." I told him good night, and gave him a kiss.

I hadn't eaten in the past 24 hours. When I got out of class, I stopped to get a quick bite to eat. I spent no more than 5 minutes. As I passed through the hall, to go up to the hospital, the phone rang. We never answered the phone, because you could spend half an hour looking for someone. I picked it up. It was for me. It was Sister Regan and said I needed to come up to the ward right away. When I got there, there was a screen around Gramp's bed, but I could see his feet under the covers.

She took me into her office and told me Gramp slept peacefully from the time I left then died just after 7:30pm. All I could think was; if I hadn't stopped to eat I would have been with him. I told her this. She said that he wouldn't have known, and he knew how much I loved him, and for me not to feel that way. She said for me not to see him, just remember him as he was. A doctor came in and said they would like to do a post-mortem. I told him I thought that would be fine, because both Gran and Gramp believed in that kind of thing. He told me that Gran had to sign a consent form. I told him, that for me to get there and back the same day would be impossible, because there weren't any buses. They arranged for a taxi to take me home and bring me back.

The whole family was at Gran's when I got there. Having to tell them that Gramp had died, and that they wanted to do a post-mortem was not an easy thing for me to do. Gran signed the consent. The rest of the family was very upset. I tried to console them, but explained I had to get back with the consent. Denis came out with me, and said someone is going to have to make the funeral arrangements. He asked me if I could meet him at Trinder's the next day, and maybe between the two of us we could get it done. He didn't think the others could handle it. I told him I would. They did let me have the time off, to meet him the next day.

When I returned to the hospital with the consent, the doctor asked me if I wanted to be in on the post-mortem. I said; "are you asking me if I want to watch my grandfather's post-mortem?" He said yes. I told him I did not, and I did not think it was very considerate of him asking me such a thing. To this day I have never watched a PM, and come to that I never intend to. I still think he was a mercenary bastard. His post-mortem showed he had a primary cancer of his stomach, with metastasis to his liver, to the extent that it was white. There was not a piece of normal liver tissue left. Yet he had no signs of jaundice or ascites.

I met Denis at Trinder's the next day, and we were able to make all the arrangements. The only problem was that the funeral was to be on the

Saturday, that I was supposed to leave on a week's holiday with Mousey. It had all been paid for, even the bus fare. I said I would see if someone else could take my place with Mousey. Later that evening, when I got home, the family said they had been talking, and they all felt that I should go on holiday, especially Gran. They said that I needed the rest, and I had been there for all of them, and for Gramp, when it was needed the most. They could manage the funeral. It was the least they could do. Gran then said; your Gramp would have wanted it this way. So I did. At 1pm, just at the same time that Gramp's funeral was taking place in Aynhoe, the bus we were on stopped for a funeral procession that was passing by. I cried.

Chapter 5

Early Student Years

Now that I have explained briefly what our training involved, I will share some of the many memories during those years. These memories tend to stay with you. Some are worth sharing, some are funny, some are sad, whilst others are enlightening or just plain crazy, you can be the judge!

Going back to Holbech Ward, after school, was comforting, plus with it being familiar ground, even the added responsibilities didn't seem so scary. Although there was one scary incident, which quickly made me realize just how dangerous a simple T & A can be. Tonsils and adenoids are a very quick surgery, as mentioned earlier when I had mine removed (See previous book). In those days the child was put under, by what is called 'dropping ether' for the anaesthetic. Then, in less than two minutes the adenoids are removed first using a snare type instrument, and the tonsils using a guillotine instrument. The latter has a hole at the end, with a blade in the shaft, that when the hole is over the tonsil, the trigger mechanism snaps the blade across the base of it. First one tonsil, then the other; both are out within seconds. Obviously there is some bleeding, but for the most part it clots very quickly, and the child wakes up with a sore throat. This probably sounds strange or cruel, but if the child eats a dry cereal, such as corn flakes with milk on it, for their first meal, after the second mouthful the soreness goes away. If they eat the traditional ice cream, the pain will be there a long time.

The tonsil drives at the Horton, were not like the ones in Oxford. Ours tonsil drives usually only numbered 6-8 children at a time. As soon as the surgery was finished, they were brought back to the ward. Each nurse was responsible for two patients at a time, to monitor their return to consciousness and physical status. Most especially to watch for any excessive bleeding, and that they maintained a clear airway. During one of these times I had an eleven year old girl I was monitoring who, just the week before, had learned she had passed the eleven plus exam, and would be going on to grammar school.

She was doing fine. She had come out of the anaesthetic without any problems, and had no signs of bleeding; her colour was good. When, suddenly she went blue. I grabbed her shoulder and pulled her head towards me and down, so that gravity could help bring forward whatever was blocking her airway. At the same time I used the suction in her mouth to try and get out whatever was there. It sucked out a huge clot, that must have formed way in the back of her throat until it completely blocked her airway. Her colour came back to normal immediately, and she responded fine. I was shaking. It felt like the emergency had lasted forever. Sister Stewart said I did everything right. She saw it happening from the bottom of the patient's bed, but by the time she got to the head of the bed to help me, I had got it all back to normal. She said it only took me a matter of seconds. I asked her why I didn't notice something was wrong beforehand. She said it rarely shows until it gets to this situation, that is why it is so important to watch T & A's so closely. I have always had great respect for this so called 'simple surgery' ever since. It took me longer to get over the shaking from it. Sister said that was from the adrenaline surge I had when it happened, but that I should be proud of myself.

There is one thing you notice very quickly, working with children. They can be deathly sick one day, and you work with them constantly to try and turn them around. Then in no time at all they are well, and jumping around in their cot as if nothing was ever wrong. Their resilience is incredible.

There wasn't a rush to get patients out of the hospital, before they were completely well. So we kept the large ward for the children that were getting close to going home. There were plenty of toys and games for them to play with, and when the weather was good we had a protected garden spot for them to play in. On the days when the weather wasn't so good, trying to keep them entertained took a little more effort. The children were dressed in day clothes each day. The ward had a large supply of clothes in all different sizes, all laundered in the hospital laundry.

This was 1958, and Rock and Roll music was very popular - especially Elvis Presley. We had a radio in the ward, and usually kept it on a music station. One day we were having an especially difficult time keeping the kids entertained. Sister and Staff nurse had gone to lunch, and there were just a couple of us student nurses on the ward. The radio was playing several Elvis songs, and the kids kept asking us to dance to it for them. The dance that was done to this was called jiving. We finally said we would dance just one for them, with the next song, and that was it. The next one was "Don't Be Cruel." We danced it for them, and just as we got to the last twirl around, who should walk into the ward but Sister and Matron. We were told to go to her office and to think about what we were doing.

In her office we tried to convince her that this was a one-time thing and why we were doing it. She wasn't convinced. We were behaving undignified, etc. etc. and she would be watching our performances very closely from now on.

These early years it took a lot of nursing skills to cure patients, especially since antibiotics were still almost non-existent. All we had was penicillin. It was used very sparingly, for only the sickest patients, because they were very concerned if we used it for everything, as they did in America, people might build up a resistance to it. Then, when they really needed it, it would have no affect on them. For the same reason, when we administered it, we had to wear a mask and sterile gloves. This was in case we built up a resistance to it ourselves, by over-exposure from handling it. The penicillin was treated like gold. It was kept in a locked cooling chest in the middle of the hospital. To get it out, two nurses had to be present, and when the bottle was removed each nurse had to sign for it. Each bottle had a number on it that was written on the form; then the time it was removed, for which patients it was to be used for, and our names. Each bottle had several doses in it. It was in powder form and a sterile liquid was added to it to dissolve it. It was always given intramuscularly and deep into the muscle. The same two nurses that got the bottle, had to stay with it, until it had all been administered to the patients it was listed for. This meant the two nurses went to each bedside, to see that the patient received it. Then both nurses had to sign the patients' chart, to show that it had been administered. When this had been completed, the same two nurses returned the empty bottle to the same cooler, to put the bottle into the used container so it could be accounted for. Of course, the form on the front of the cooler was signed again, to show it had been completed. Penicillin was monitored even more tightly, than for the administration for narcotics.

The first adult ward I was assigned to, after the children's ward, was the men's surgical/orthopaedics ward - C-Ward. Sister Andrew-Arthur was the sister in charge of this ward. She was very easy to get along with. So long as you did your work well, she left you alone. As with all the wards, during our first year we spent more time cleaning, especially in the utility room, than anything else. But because it wasn't medical patients, there wasn't quite the volume. So we were able to get out and do other things much earlier in the day.

This turned out to be a double-edged sword for me. The problem was that the wards were very large, with sixteen beds on one side and twenty on the other, of this very long and wide room. Down the centre of the ward were armchairs, and a large dining table with chairs. The sickest patients were kept in the first four beds, on the side with twenty beds. Opposite these four beds, the private and amenity rooms were located. As one entered the ward, the medicine room was to the left, and the sterile room was on the right. The patients with orthopaedic problems were kept at the far end of the ward, because they were usually "well," just taking longer to heal, requiring longer lengths of stay.

    I did fine as long as I didn't have to go into the large open part of the ward. As soon as I left this safe zone, then my trouble started, and I found out how shy I was. The patients would start off by calling to each other: "We have a new nurse starting." Then they would proceed to talk loudly to each other about you, as if you could neither hear nor see them. I would get no further than three steps into the ward, and I would start turning red. I had absolutely no idea what my legs, or any other part of my body, were doing. If I had to put a screen around a bed, to treat a patient, the teasing got even worse.

    Bearing in mind our uniforms were very modest, with hem lines just fourteen inches from the floor, dresses and aprons made of linen, then thick black stockings and lace up walking shoes. The only thing that was showing of us was our faces, hands and arms. The whole time I was inside the ward, my face, hands, and arms were bright red. Then this one patient yelled out: "Look! Her arms and face are still red. I bet her legs are too if we could see behind those thick stockings of hers." I was about ready to collapse from total embarrassment, when this one patient signalled he wanted to talk to me. I went over to him and he asked me to put the screen around him. While I was doing this, there were loud comments about how lucky he was.

    After I put the screen around his bed, I asked him what he needed. He said he wanted to just talk to me, without everyone listening. I really couldn't see how the screen would make much difference. He then told me he thought the teasing had gone on long enough, and he had asked the other patients to slow down; that it was getting out of hand. He said they were enjoying it too much to listen to reason. So the only way to stop it was for me to not let it bother me. I said; I didn't know how to do that. He told me that, before I step into the large part of the ward, to glance down the length of it, to make sure there was nothing for me to trip over; then to fix my eyes on something up ahead, at the far end of the ward, and count backwards slowly, concentrating on the counting as I walked. He said this way you will be able to block out the comments, then you won't blush, thereby giving them no reason to keep teasing me. I was very sceptical that this would work, but it did. The teasing soon stopped when they weren't able to get any pleasure out of it. In the end they turned out to be a great bunch of patients. One of them even gave me this note of apology; I have kept it all these years:

"If, owing to my poor powers of verbal expression,
any slight to your honourable person was conceived
I pray for your forgiveness."
John C. Bushell.

He was a school teacher by profession.

Whilst I was on C-Ward for the first time, Denis, my uncle, had to have an inguinal hernia repair. He was so concerned that I would be the one to have to shave him, and give him a bed bath after surgery. He did not believe me that we weren't allowed to treat relatives, until another nurse went to his bed to do it for him.

Lord Saye 'n Sele came into the private room for surgery during my time there. He was probably in his seventies at the time. He was extremely nice, and not at all demanding. In fact, as soon as he was over the worst of his surgery, he was very independent and spent most of his time out in the main ward, visiting with the other patients and playing games with them. He said that if he has to come into the hospital again, he wasn't going to be shut up in that private room. He was going to be out in the ward where all the action was. It is true that the large wards are very lively places, not at all places to feel lonely in.

The other positive thing about large wards, is the camaraderie between them all. They give each other support, encouragement and education, on what to expect and how quickly they will get better. This support extends into the families as well; it is not unusual to develop lifetime friendships from these hospital stays. The families benefited, because the visiting times were set times each day, without exceptions. So the families got to know each other as well, and often associated with each other, while the family member was in the hospital.

One observation we nurses made, that held true through all the years, was the personality and behaviour of the patients before, during, and after visiting times. It went like this with rare exception:

On the men's ward, when it is not visiting hours, they are lively, talkative, joking, and generally having a good time, rarely demanding of the nurses unless they are very sick. About fifteen minutes before visiting time starts, the change starts to take place. They start hunkering down in their beds, with this 'pity me' look on their faces. As soon as the visitors get to are suffering. They lap up all the petting, spoiling and condolences they can get. Before the last person has left the ward, the transformation is instant, and they are back to their usual jovial selves. Their families leave, especially the wives, worried sick.

On the women's ward, the medical being worse than the surgical ward, probably because they are sicker, it is totally different. All day long they are demanding they can never get enough care or compassion, and they complain constantly between each other; each one trying to outdo the other, as to the seriousness of their condition. There is no such thing as being able to uplift them. Then thirty minutes before visiting, the transformation takes place. The special nightie comes out, that is saved for visiting time, with the pretty bed jacket to compliment the gown. Hair is fixed, so one would think they had just visited the hairdressers, and the makeup goes on. They are sitting upright in bed, with smiles on their, faces ready to welcome all that come. Not a complaint comes out of their mouths; they are all smiles and full of laughs. As soon as the last visitor leaves the ward, the special nightie and makeup are off. Their countenance changes and they are back to the complaints and demands. Except they have updated information to share with each other. The visitors, especially husbands, leave wondering why they are still in the hospital, and not home taking care of them. I found it fascinating to watch.

The large wards all had many windows, and glass French doors every two beds down the side of the ward. When the weather was nice, we would wheel the beds outside, for the ones that couldn't get out of bed. This way they could get some fresh air. For the others we would just move chairs outside for them. The only problem with the men's surgical, was that they all wanted to go out on the left side, because it faced the garden of the nurses' home. There was more activity for them to see! We did seem to come up with enough space for them all.

It was during this time we had a new student start. She was unusual, even for us. The middle of the afternoon, on her first day working, she could not be found anywhere. After searching everywhere, someone went into the linen room to get something, and found her there fast asleep on a pile of blankets. Her explanation was; I always take a nap in the afternoon. She was told; not anymore you don't. She turned out to be totally clueless. Trying to find jobs for her to do, that didn't create more work for ourselves, was nigh on impossible. We asked her to take all the patient thermometers and clean them. This was taught in class before coming out onto the wards. The thermometers were kept in glass tubes, held in brackets that were attached to the walls behind each patient's bed. There was a piece of cotton wool in the bottom of each tube, with an antiseptic solution in it, to protect and keep the thermometer clean. All she had to do was; take all the containers down, scrub the tubes, replace the cotton and antiseptic solution, put the thermometer that had been washed in alcohol back in them, and re-hang them on the wall. Instead, she gathered everything up in a large basin, and poured the hottest water she could, from the tap, over everything. All the thermometers were broken, and some of the tubes, but with all that mercury floating loose none of it could be used. The next major thing she did was; she was to go around to each patient and clean their teeth. At this time most of our patients had false teeth. After she had cleaned them all, she came to us with this large basin, with all these gleaming teeth staring up at us. She wanted to know what she was to do with them now!! We had to take the basin first to the most "with it" patients, to see if they recognized their own teeth. Let me tell you, there was a lot of trial and error over the next 24 hours. A lot was by process of elimination. I do not remember if she ever finished her training.

Nurses in those days, had quite a few superstitions; one of which was, that it was bad luck it give a patient red and white flowers. The florists in Banbury knew, always to put one single flower, of another colour, in with it. The superstition was, that the colours represented the red and white corpuscles, and if given this way, there would be a death in the ward. Both John Burden, another student nurse I was working with at the time, and I thought it was a stupid superstition, and we were going to prove it wrong. I was doing the general ward flowers most of the following week, so I could easily pot the colours together, and discretely place them in the ward. This was a surgical ward, so they have fewer deaths than the medical floors. So, for close to a week, a vase had just red and white flowers in it. Every day we had a death on the ward. For John and me that was a bit too much. A few days later I was doing the flowers, and happened to glance at the ones I had finished, and noticed there was one with just red and white flowers in it. I grabbed those flowers and threw them into the tub with all the others, just to break them up. I had no sooner done that, when John came down to me, and you'll never guess what just happened! Mr. J just died. He was supposed to be going home that day. I told John and said I felt like I had killed him.

The area around Banbury is mainly farming country, and so we usually got our fair share of farming accidents. One in particular was an incredible story. In the autumn, the farms are busy getting the grain crops in, and the combine harvester earns its keep during this time. We got word that there was a fifteen year old coming in, who had got his leg caught in the combine. Just below his knee, his leg was only held on with about an inch of flesh. He was being brought straight to the ward, to be prepped as much as possible, then going straight to surgery. Our casualty officer, Dr Yankovitch, was going to perform the surgery, and he was going to try and re-attach it. They thought he stood a better chance of success, the quicker it was done, rather than send him to Oxford, or to wait for one of the orthopaedists to come to Banbury.

I saw the leg before he went to surgery. It was in shreds where the amputation took place. The kid was an excellent footballer, and the hope was that he would eventually still be able to play. They were in surgery the best part of eight hours. The theatre nurses said it was incredible to watch Dr Yankovitch. He was so careful and so patient, patching and re-attaching muscles and nerves together. It was like an incredible jig saw puzzle going together. Then he cast the whole leg, and said he would have to bring him back to surgery, initially a couple of times a week, to remove the cast and debride it and re-dress it. Debriding is when it is necessary to remove tissue, whether it is skin, fat or muscle, that has died or sloughed off. If this isn't removed, then it will cause more to die off. It is removed until you can see good healthy regenerating tissue. What is really happening to the tissue, is it is healing from the inside out. This is indeed what happened, and it went on for weeks, before he could go to weekly trips to the theatre for dressing changes. The next week, when the Oxford orthopaedic surgeon was visiting Banbury, he told Yankovitch that the surgery wouldn't work; he was wasting time. The boy would eventually lose his leg anyway. Dr Yankovitch said the boy, and his family, were willing to try to save his leg, and he was willing to invest the time. It took months - almost a year - but it worked, and when he left the hospital extensive physiotherapy was still needed. I saw him a couple of years later, and he wasn't even limping, and he was playing football again. He said he did limp a bit when he was very tired, but that was all.

We had another patient admitted, who had been in a motor bike accident. As I mentioned in my first book, there are nasty bends in the road all the way through Aynhoe. Well this one happened on the bend in the road, coming from Bicester onto the Croughton Road. It was dark, the road was wet, and he lost control of the bike and went off the road into a ditch. He said he didn't feel any particular pain. He just knew he had to get out of the ditch, because it was filling up with water from all the rain. So he grabbed on to a branch to pull himself up. When cars headlights flashed onto him, he saw that what he had thought was a branch ,and he was pulling himself up with was, in actuality, his femur that was protruding through his trousers. He said that at first he couldn't believe it, because he felt no pain. He said the next car spotted him, stopped and got an ambulance. He said that he never felt any pain, until after he came out of the effects of the anaesthesia. He was in the military, stationed at Aldershot. When he was stable enough to be transferred to the army hospital there, he went by ambulance. I had to go with him. We had to go through Aynhoe, so I was able to show him where he had his accident. He said the next time through Aynhoe, no matter what the weather conditions, he was going to go at a snails pace.

Christmas at the Horton - my first Christmas working on the wards was going to be on C-Ward, just before I was due to be changed to B-Ward, - women's medical.

On Christmas day no-one is allowed to be off duty. We worked either a twelve-hour day or night shift. We are there to make Christmas as enjoyable as we possible can for the patients. Each ward has a head physician or surgeon. They were expected to, and did participate in this, with very special duties. Their wives and children were also expected to attend, along with the town Mayor and his or her family.

Preparation for Christmas starts weeks ahead. Each ward or department has to be decorated in a special theme, all of which is made by the staff and patients, and is kept top secret from all the other wards. Whatever the theme is, then a costume has to be made, for the head physician or surgeon to wear, while he carves the turkey and serves it to each patient. This is followed by the Christmas pudding. The rest of the meal is served to each of the patients by the doctor's family members, and the head nurses on the floor. Between courses, while the patients are eating, the doctor is expected to entertain the patients appropriately, according to what their costume dictates. Lots of fun was had by all.

The themes varied incredibly. The children's ward usually had pantomime themes, such as Dick Whittington, Aladdin or Cinderella. The adult wards could be anything from pirates to Robinson Crusoe. In the later years, and with the start of the space age, they even got into that. My last Christmas at the Horton, I was working in the operating theatre. All we could decorate there was Sister's office, so we did it as a witches cave with stalagmites etc. And a menu for witches brew, that incorporated all the nurses and surgeons names, that were working there at the time. (See the picture of the verse). The patients had full Christmas dinners. The nurses got cold cuts and pickles, but most of us didn't bother to go to the dining room to eat. The private rooms on each floor were turned into a room for all donated snacks - food and drinks - which was laid out for the nurses. During this time of the year, the donations to the nurses were incredible. Each ward would receive so much, that it could have stocked a store and an off license with the food, wine and liqueur. Yes, on Christmas Day, all staff were allowed to drink alcohol on duty, but to drink sensibly. Staff from all the wards would visit others to admire or comment on the decorations, and each one who visited would be invited into the "nurses' room" to share refreshments. No one drank too much it was all very proper and dignified. Patients and visitors were also allowed alcohol to drink, as long as there was nothing wrong with them that it could cause a problem, or as long as they were not too young. In Britain, the legal drinking age was 17 if someone else buys it for you, and 18 for you to be able to buy it.

Visiting for patient's friends and family, was all day after about 11:00 am, which was to give us enough time to get everything done for the patients. This way they could just relax and have fun. Most of the patients and families said it was more fun than being at home. In fact some of our NFA (no fixed abode) patients, used to plan on being in the hospital for Christmas. They used to come up with some incredible complaints, so as to guarantee getting in.

Our daytime work hours on this day, were from 7:30 am to 7:30pm. Then we could go off duty. At the same time, families were leaving with plans to rest up on Boxing Day. My first Christmas away from home, Mum and Dad were in one of their fighting, no talking modes, so Dad was on his own for Christmas. Life at the Rehab hospital had changed, with very few patients' left. Those that were still there, were going home for Christmas. Therefore Dad had arranged to take me out to dinner, at the Whately Hall Hotel, on Christmas Day evening. He said he would pick me up at 7:45 pm, and that I needed to be dressed in at least a cocktail dress. I wore a medium blue princess line dress, with a "V" neck line, sleeveless with a very full gored skirt and, as was all the rage then, several lace petticoats under it, to make the skirt stand out in a very feminine fashion. To finish it off, a pair of white pointed toed shoes, with 4-inch high spike heels, and of course white gloves. In those days, one would not dream of going out without wearing gloves. I had learned a long time before, how to change from uniform into party clothes, complete with makeup, in less than ten minutes. It is a matter of having everything laid out and ready for you, so no time is wasted. Organization is everything.

It turned out to be not just a dinner, but a Christmas dinner with party games after, for all the guests that were there, which was about thirty people, plus the staff. The tables were set very graciously with white linen, silver cutlery and bone china; including very decorative Christmas centre pieces on each table, which we were allowed to take home at the end of the evening. The serving table had turkeys, all golden brown, and ready for the chef to carve, along with all the accruements steaming hot. Dad and I each had a glass of sherry along with our starters, wine with our main course, followed by Christmas puddings that were brought into the darkened dining room, flaming in the traditional custom; served with hard sauce, coffee and brandy with a cheese plate on the side. Following the leisurely dinner, the tables were cleared for the party games that lasted till midnight. Prizes were given out for all the games, and Christmas crackers were in abundance, to be shared with fellow guests. It was all most unexpected and lots of fun. Dad told me he had told Matron where he was taking me, and unbeknown to me, I had been granted a special pass to stay out past the usual pass hours. It was a very special Christmas, for the first one of many that we nurses are required to do; having to work over Christmas.

At the start of the New Year, I had the rude awakening of working on the female medical ward - "B-Ward", as a first year student. Oh my God! Talk about reality orientation! If a student nurse can survive that exposure, they can survive anything, and they really want to be a nurse.

If student nurses of today, were given that kind of exposure early in their student days, there would not be the drop out of nursing as we see it today, after they have graduated and started working on the wards. Student nurses today are so protected, with absolutely no idea what the job really entails; to work a full shift, or a double shift, with patients that they haven't been able to select because they are "interesting." They do not seem to get the education nowadays, that they would get working with common or chronic diseases. The chronically ill patients, with the common disease entities are the norm, and there are very many of them. The art is to treat each patient as if their problem is unique, as it is to them, and afford them all the care skills and TLC they are entitled to, even though they may be one of twenty you have to take care of. The students of today, that I have seen in America, can select 2 or 3 to take care of, for 3-5 hours a day, as their required patient exposure, lasting no more than a few weeks. This in my book, borders on cruelty to both the nurse, because she has no idea about what work is really like, and to the patients they are expected to be caring, and are responsible for once they have graduated.

Let's return to B-Ward in 1959. This is a ward full of very ill women, ranging in age from eighteen to whenever; we had a lot more of the whenever. The set up in the ward was the same as all the others, as was described in the men's surgical ward. The only difference with this one, was that the last two beds, at the far end of each side of the ward, had a solid wall partition. These were used for ill nurses that needed hospital care. Though most of the time, they were used for the less ill regular patients just before being discharged. When we were loaded, with a ward full of very ill patients, those were used for them. Just the doors were left open. It is not unusual for the ward to be short of beds, even with the 36 that were there, and we would have to move the tables and chairs out of the centre of the ward, to put extra beds up. That could hold an additional 4 beds; bringing the total to 42, counting the private and amenity rooms.

The normal staffing for days, to cover the ward and to include days off, was; 1 sister, 1 senior staff nurse, 1 junior staff nurse, 1 third year, 2 second year and 3 first year student nurses. The hours to be covered by these few staff was; from 7:30 am to 8:30pm. Luckily for staffing, we all only had one day off a week. But during those daytime hours one each of the qualified nurses, and one of the student nurses, would be off from 10:00 am to 2:00 pm, and another would be off from 2:00 pm to 5:00 pm. One qualified nurse and two student nurses would work from 7:30 am until 6:00 pm. They used to like to have the person scheduled to be off at 6 pm, the day before their day off.

Nights were covered by 1 sister, who oversaw all the wards, 1 third year student, 1 second year student, and 1 of one of the following, a first year student, an orderly (nurses aide) or a SEAN. These were nurses who had had two years of education, and had taken exams for that level of care. Nights we worked from 8:00 pm to 8:00 am. Again we only had 1 night off a week. It was really tough if you had the Sunday off one week and the Saturday off the next week, meaning you worked 12 nights straight to just to have one night off again. This was a killer. We were not allowed to sit down at all while on duty during the day shifts, but on nights we were permitted to sit down to do our paperwork. After the patients were settled down for the night, we would make a circle of screens in the middle of the ward, arrange a small table and armchairs for ourselves, and use goose neck floor lamps to give us light, to work without disturbing the patients. We were located there so we could hear the patients when they called out to us.

The first year students on B-Ward, spent almost all their time in the utility room cleaning bedpans, and testing urine and stools. Doing the bedpan rounds 3 times a day and whenever needed, making beds and giving bed baths to the bed bound patients. Changing sputum cups and mopping up sputum that had been accidentally knocked over by someone. That was my Achilles heals! I could handle anything that was offered for me to do, but mopping up sputum was something else. I would be retching the whole time. Every time the mop was placed on the sputum, and you tried to pull it up, it would string from the mop to the floor and not let go. It was almost too much. The odour didn't help any either. We had bonuses, in as much that we could get out of the utility room, for cleaning the linen and storage rooms, and the kitchen after the meals were served. On rare occasions, we were allowed to help with passing out meals, and feeding the patients that needed to be fed. We were also given the privilege of cleaning up all the incontinent patients, and to do it with a smile and kind words to the patient, so they could maintain their dignity.

In these days, the only real treatment we had for patients that had heart attacks, was total bed rest. I am sure medication was given to them also, but my level of knowledge at that time did not extend to what was being administered. The bed rest was to the extent, that the patient was not allowed to do anything for themselves. From wiping their nose to turning over in the bed. We did absolutely everything for them. The idea was that with total rest, it would give the heart a chance to heal. There was no knowledge, that being sedentary for that long, would encourage the development of blood clots in the vascular system. We were doing what was considered the treatment of choice at the time. Neither did we know about CPR - Cardiac Pulmonary Resuscitation.

There was one patient during this time on B-Ward, I remember very well. She had been admitted following a coronary, as we called a heart attack in those days. She was in her early forties, and even as ill as she was when she was first admitted, and the restrictions put on her with the treatment needed, she never complained. She was patient and not at all demanding. She was always positive and constantly trying to cheer everyone else up. She progressed very well, and after 4 weeks of total care, it was determined her heart was healing, and she could be graduated up into increasing her activity and independence. This was done very gradually, with the expected outcome being, that she would be ready for discharge in about another 3 weeks. As she improved, she continued to be the same kind of patient as she was early on, but now she would go around the ward cheering everyone else up. She had an exceptional sense of humour, and could tell stories, to keep the patients in fits of laughter, most of the time. The day before she was to be discharged, she was sitting up in bed telling one of her stories. Everyone was laughing, and someone came back with a remark, that set her off laughing as much as everyone else. In the middle of it all, she had a massive heart attack and died. The ward was never happy again. Everyone she had touched was devastated.

    At the end of our 12 weeks of working on B-Ward, the other student nurses were rotated off, but I wasn't. It was almost like I was forgotten. The other strange thing was, the five student nurses that replaced the others were all from the same class, and from the class just two before mine, so they had just gone into their second year. Bearing in mind how the jobs were delegated, according to the student's level in training, problems loomed ahead. Especially since Sister Cook was the kind that was very wishy-washy, and told the students to decide between themselves who did what. Well, let me tell you; no-one was going to volunteer to do the menial tasks, and let their other classmates do the jobs of the higher ranking students. They fought constantly. The staff nurses on the ward were no better than Sister Cook, for stepping in and taking charge. So, you know who got left doing all the menial work; the one that was still a first year student, namely me. I put up with this for two weeks, with no signs of me being transferred to another ward.

    The weekly ward cleaning day was raising its ugly head again, and I wasn't going to be stuck like I was the previous week, doing it all while they fought amongst themselves. So I climbed out of my bedroom window and caught the early bus to Oxford, knowing full well when I got there, there would be a telegram telling my mother to send me back. Which of course she would. But, by the time I got back, the ward cleaning would be over and those other students would have had to do it.

    I will explain what weekly ward cleaning involved: but first let me set the scene for this particular time, and it had been this way for about two weeks. The ward was full of patients, plus the 4 extra beds were up in the middle. Of these 40 patients, only one could get out of bed, and then only with assistance. So obviously they all required total care, including bedpans every 2-3 hours, or bed changes because of incontinence. Now; for what the ward cleaning entailed. All of the beds had to be pushed to one side of the ward, so the high dusting could be done, without dust falling on the beds. The radiators were the old fashioned coil radiators. These were behind the heads of the beds, and they had to be individually scrubbed. Then the medicated sand was thrown onto the floor, so dust wouldn't fly, and then swept up; followed by the floors being scrubbed with an electric scrubber. This was done by a porter. While the porter was doing the scrubbing, we had the back end of the beds that were visible to clean; they were lifted on to blocks so we could scrape and scrub the wheels. Remembering of course, during this time, the patients' are still in their beds. When the first side of the ward is done, then it is repeated on the other side. When the beds are back in their regular places, the same is done through the middle of the ward, and the bottom of the bed wheels are done for both sides. After which all the furniture that remains in the centre of the ward is polished. As you can imagine, when there are four additional beds in the middle of the ward, it adds to the difficulty.

The week before, when all these students were arguing as to who was going to do the different jobs, with none of them wanting to do what they thought was beneath them, I was stuck with it all. Sister always took the morning off on ward cleaning day. The staff nurse hid in sister's office all morning. Incidentally, she was the same staff nurse that used the bathroom that caused me to get dysentery!

I enjoyed my bus ride to Oxford, more than any time before or since. Of course, everything was as predicted. The telegram was there. Mum asked me what was going on, and I told her. She didn't pass any opinion, but she did tell me I should have lunch before I went back. The telegram said I was to go to Matrons office when I returned. I did have the bus ride back to think about that, and to plan what I was going to say to her.

Dutifully I went to Matrons office and she took me to another office. She asked me why I did what I did. So I explained to her about the student nurse situation, and how unfair it was. Adding that I did not like working on B-Ward. She said that Medical wards were the hardest to work on, but that a "true nurse" would enjoy it. I looked her straight in the eye and told her: "Then I can't be a true nurse, because I hate it. In any case, my contract for training was to rotate through the wards twelve weeks at a time, and I have been on B-Ward fourteen weeks; which is beyond what is required of me." She just looked at me, and didn't say anything for what seemed an eternity. Then she told me to go back to the nurses' home, and to report to her office in the morning, to find out where I was to go. The following morning I was told I was to finish out the week on B-Ward, and to start my night's rotation at the Elms the following week. In all fairness to Matron, she never put me back on to a medical floor, until my third year as a student. I didn't mind one bit.

There was another situation, concerning Matron, that I had to deal with, that did not affect any of the other nurses. Her surname name was Alford, mine was Alsford. Because of this she was constantly getting my post, though it is strange I never got hers! Her maid would always hand carry my post to me from Matron, with a note attached to it stating she had opened it by mistake! It was maybe how she knew more about what was going on in my life, than she did any of the other nurses.

The Elms: obstetrics and nights. With the start of night duty, we moved our bedroom to the night staff corridor in the nurse's home. It was shut off from the rest of the rooms, to promote quietness, making it easier for the nurses to sleep. It was upstairs, so there was no escaping out of your bedroom window if things got too tough!

The Elms was as different from B-Ward, as chalk is from cheese. At one time it must have been some wealthy person's home, because it was more like a mansion. It had a grand, sweeping staircase into the main entrance hall of the house. Two large rooms in the back of the house were nurseries for the newborn babies. They had large windows and were very pleasant, quiet rooms, except when the babies were crying - if one cries they all cry!

Left of the front door was a large room, that had 5 beds in it for mothers. These were ones that would be going home in the next 2 to 3 days. Mothers stayed in the hospital 10 days after delivery. Most of them were first time mothers, because after the first babies, if there were no problems with the delivery, the district nurses, all of whom were midwives, delivered the babies at home. We only had the other mothers, if there had been problems with an earlier delivery, or that it was decided the mother needed the rest.

The room to the right of the stairs, was a very large, pleasant staff room, beautifully furnished with desks, armchairs, and a dining room table and chairs. There was a fireplace in this room as well. The fully equipped kitchen for the house was large, and in the back of the house. All the meals for the patients and staff were prepared here. The food was much better than the hospital food. The orderly prepared the night staff food; she was an excellent cook. We used to have our dinner as close to 1am as we could. That was dependent on what was happening with the patients, bearing in mind most babies seem to be delivered at night. The only other staff working at night, besides the student nurse, was the midwife, and she was a sister. The one I worked with the most, during my time there, was Sister Anderson. She was a good teacher, very caring and considerate towards her patients and staff. She treated me as if I was human. It was a nice change after B-Ward.

Upstairs there were 3 large rooms used as wards. Each held about 8 beds, an office / treatment room, and four large bathrooms with treatment tables in. Then down 3 steps, and along a hallway, were 2 more bathrooms and two delivery rooms. In the basement were the laundry and a drying room. My first job each night, was to wash all the nappies from the daytime. There was an electric copper to boil them in, once I had washed them clean. Then they were rinsed, run through the ringer, and hung to dry in the drying room. In the morning they would be dry, required folding and placed in the airing cupboard. When we were full, it was nothing for me to have well over 100 nappies to wash.

My other duties were to help the midwife with the mothers and babies. I would be responsible for the mothers' episiotomies care; douches and breast care post delivery. I would take the babies to the mothers each morning, after the midwife had bathed them, for feeding. If the babies were bottle-fed, we fed them during the night, so the mothers could get a good nights sleep. Most of the babies were bottle-fed at the time. That always seemed to go in waves.

When a patient was admitted in labour at nighttime, they were taken upstairs to one of the bathrooms, and examined by the midwife to see how far along she was. Husbands or family members did not stay around. They were told to call in the morning, to find out how she was doing.

After sister had examined her, she would tell me to shave and give her an enema, if it was ok. Sometimes they were too far along to give an enema, which could put the baby or mother at risk. Sister used to say; we don't need to see a baby's face, looking up at us from inside the commode, because she delivered it while passing the enema. Those that were too far along, went straight to the delivery room via stretcher. We had ramps we could put down, over the 3 steps down to the delivery room, making it possible to roll them down there.

If the mother was in early labour, after I had finished with the enema etc. sister would examine the mother, and if she had progressed far enough to go to the delivery room, then she would go down there. If not, she would go into one of the ward beds, where we would monitor her overnight. We usually had one room empty, or with other mothers at the same level, so we didn't have to disturb the ones with babies.

Some nights we wouldn't have any admissions or any deliveries, but that wasn't very often. We usually averaged one admission and two deliveries a night. Deliveries were really beautiful things. The delivery room was not a huge impersonal room. The bed was wider than hospital beds, with a firm board under a very thick comfortable mattress. There was no headboard, but rather a rail that went across the back of the bed, and about 24 inches down each side, about a foot higher than the mattress. This was for the mother to hold, or grip onto, for the pain, or to help push as the case may be. The bed was high, so the patient could transfer easily from the stretcher to the bed, and at a height that was compatible for the nurse and midwife to work, during the delivery.

Beside the bed was the tank of nitrous oxide (laughing gas) with a mask attached. This was for the mother to use, if the labour pains got to be too much. If the mother had a way to go, before she would be fully dilated and effaced, sister would give the mother a small dose of liquid chloral hydrate (a sedative). She would say; she'll sleep through the worst of it, will wake up ready to go when she is fully dilated, and will have the energy to push when it is time, instead of wasting her energy on the labour pains. I never saw it fail.

When the mother was ready to push, the patient would lie on her side facing me, put her right foot on my left shoulder, hold one of my hands with her right hand, and hold the rail with her left hand. She could have used the gas if she had wanted, but usually all she wants to do is push and not mess with the gas. Using my shoulder, my hand and the rail, she would use all for leverage to push or squeeze, if the pain was too much. The midwife was on the other side of the bed to deliver the baby.

Those babies would pop out so fast, and as pink as you like, screaming bloody murder! The mother would turn onto her back, and hold the baby for a while, until she was ready to pass the placenta. That was usually done with her lying on her back. After the placenta was passed, she was injected with the pitocin, to slow down the bleeding. Sister would massage her uterus, to get it to tighten back up, and then take the baby down to the nursery to clean it up etc. I would clean up the mother, check her vital signs, and make her comfortable in the bed.

When the mother was comfortable, I would go down to the kitchen and prepare the post delivery refreshment tray for her. This was a wooden tray with a starched white lace cloth on it, a matching bone china tea plate, cup and saucer, silver bread knife and teaspoon, along with silver teapot, small milk jug and sugar bowl, finished with a lace serviette. There was fresh tea in the pot, and the plate held two slices of buttered toast with the crusts cut off, and sliced into a delicate finger shape. If we had fresh flowers, we would have a posy in a vase on the tray. This was taken to the new Mum, and she was told what a great job she had done, the baby was doing fine, and she deserved a special treat. The mothers loved it. They said it made them feel so special, and it was just enough to refresh them. It just hit the right spot.

One night, when we came on duty, we found we had 3 mums in hard labour. We had no empty beds for any more admissions. Luckily, by that time, I had been working there about eight weeks, so I was fairly competent in what I did, and I knew the routine. There is no way I can describe the real extent of how the night progressed. Rather I will give it the best way I can. We had 4 admissions, all in various stages of labour. Two of these were moving along very rapidly, so I shaved them and put them straight into the delivery rooms. The other two I shaved and gave them their enemas. They had to stay on the examination table in each of the bathrooms, because there were no beds for them. The two in the delivery rooms, delivered in quick succession, and we moved those out. One to the third bathroom on the examination table there, whilst the other stayed on the stretcher in the hall. I rapidly cleaned up both delivery rooms, for two of the Mums that were admitted earlier, that were moving right along. They had to walk to the delivery rooms, because a patient was on the stretcher that had just delivered. Not an easy feat when fully dilated.

These two delivered, we got them back to their beds by carrying them, with the sister and me making a sling with our arms for them to sit in. Then one of the new admits, and the last of the Mums admitted earlier, moved right along. So again a rapid clean up of the delivery rooms and they were transferred there.

One of the new admits was a friend of my families. It was her second, but there had been a little problem with her first delivery, so there was the concern she could move along very rapidly. Both the Mums did, to the point I ended up delivering the friends baby, at the same time sister was delivering the other baby. When the babies were out, sister and I changed places so she could check the mother out. While she was doing that, both delivered their placentas, so I did a complete deliver, except it was on two different patients! Things slowed down a bit after this. We got the Mum back to the room that had a bed, and I cleaned up the friend and let her stay in the delivery room.

The orderly did the nappies that night, and fed the babies; she also made most of the special trays for the mothers after their deliveries. But there was still all the perineal and breast care to be done, babies to be bathed, and taken to the mothers. Let me tell you; I ran all night long. None of us had a chance for a drink of water, much less a meal. When the day staff came on to relieve us, they could not believe what we had gone through.

I went upstairs to the delivery room, where sister was talking to the other midwife that had come on duty, to ask her permission to go off duty. She asked me if I had eaten anything yet. I told her I hadn't, and that I didn't have the energy to eat anything. I was still going to have to walk six miles home, because I had missed my bus. This next night was my night off and Gran was expecting me. I had no way of letting her know differently. Sister said I wouldn't make it home without something, so she gave me what she called glucose tablets. They were about an inch across and flat. She said for me to suck on them as I walked along, and it would give me the energy I needed. I made it home, not remembering too much about the walk. When I got home, I just told Gran I had had a very busy night and had to get some sleep. I did not wake up until the next morning.

Newborn nursery at the Elms

Gran said she checked on me several times, to see if I was all right. She said I never moved. I can believe it. When I got back to work after my night off, sister told me how well I had worked, and that Matron had been told. She apologized for not telling me that morning, I said to her; we were all very tired by then. She agreed. I finished my night duty at the end of June, at the start of my second year, and was sent to D-Ward, the female surgical ward. To mark that occasion, we have a stripe sown on the sleeves of our uniform dresses.

The start of my second year and D-Ward women's surgical. Sister Smith ran D-Ward, she was a very strict and ran a very tight ship. She was very knowledgeable; she was also an excellent teacher. She did not like Americans and especially the girls that dated them; she thought them nothing much better than prostitutes. So, if any of the students were dating Americans, they kept it from sister. The other quirk she had, was the flowers in the ward.

When patients went home, they usually left their flowers behind for the other patients to enjoy. Sister Smith would gather them all, make large flower arrangements of them, and place them on the tables for all the patients to see. The masterpiece was a large shallow vase, that was placed on a small table, which was prominent for all to see as you walked into the ward. This arrangement was at least the width of the 3-foot table, and about 15 or more inches high. No-one - and I mean no-one, ever touched that arrangement.

With the onset of our second year of training, we had our second set of exams to take and our lectures were more frequent. Trying to fit them into our spare or off duty time, was not that easy. We had a schedule book that told us what lectures we had to attend, in any given period. It was our responsibility to meet those requirements, and to get them checked off. This continued until the last six months of my training, when they developed the study blocks for us.

Things were going along well on the ward. I was learning a lot and had more responsibility, such as doing patients dressings, removing sutures and clips, giving medications and instructing the first year students. It really works like a chain of knowledge and experience, which is passed down from one level to another. All the student nurses senior to me, were good to work for and with, as were the staff nurses. I really believe it all filters down from the top, stemming from the sister in charge.

At this time, I foolishly decided I wanted to have my hair-bleached blonde. God only knows why, because looking back on it, I can't think of any good reason for it. I finally convinced my mother to do it for me. I certainly couldn't have afforded to have it done otherwise. Mum tried to tell me it would be very hard to get it blonde, because I had so much natural red in my hair. I thought she was just trying to put me off of it. Well, eight hours, and many treatments later, she said she couldn't do anymore, otherwise my hair would fall out, I had the most orange hair you could ever wish to see.

By this time, we were getting a day and a half off a week. Sometimes it would be at the beginning of the day for the half-day, and sometimes the end. This particular time, mine was at the beginning of the day. I caught the train back to Banbury, and thought I would pick up a rinse, and put it on my hair to tone it down a bit, before I went on duty. I got a pink rinse - the worst possible colour I could have got. It made it worse. There was nothing else for it. I was going to have to go on duty the way it was.

The way the story goes, is; when I knocked on Sister Smith's office door, I poked my head in to tell her I was on duty, and left very rapidly! The nurses that were in there with her, said her mouth dropped open and she said: "What was that"? They told her they thought it was Nurse Alsford. It apparently took her some time to regain her composure. My life on the ward went downhill from there.

For the next week, I did not hear a civil word towards me from Sister Smith. I received a load of innuendoes, to suggest I was a prostitute. A blatant one was when I was waiting in the middle of the ward, for a stretcher to go past, so I could get to a patient I was with following surgery. Sister came up behind me, jabbed her finger hard into the middle of my back, and told me to move along, that I wasn't on Piccadilly Circus now. Back then all the prostitutes hung out there. I ignored her! Then I got the same remark again about Piccadilly, when I was taking care of a couple of patients that had just undergone mastectomies. I hadn't had a chance to tie one of their gowns back up at the neck, and she was very restless, thrashing her arm about so the gown came off of her shoulder. Sister came out of nowhere, grabbed her gown, and pushed it back up to her neck, with her stinging comment to me. She nit -picked everything I did. I just kept ignoring the comments, with the thought just to consider the source from whence they came.

The final straw came, when she accused me of taking a patients' walking stick. I told her I had no use for the stick, and that I had hooked it on the radiator behind the patients bed. She told me to go out of her office and return the walking stick. I asked her if she was accusing me of stealing it. She didn't respond to that, other than to say I was to get the stick back for the patient. I went back to the patient's bed, and it was where I had said it was, except it had fallen off the radiator and was just leaning against it.

By this time I was so angry with Sister, and the way she had been with me, tears were running down my cheeks from trying to control my anger. I tore a cotton handkerchief into shreds, and told the other nurses I was going to report it to Matron. They tried to stop me but there was no stopping me. I was determined.

I did the unthinkable thing, of marching straight into Matrons office with only a brief knock on her door. There I stood staring straight at her, with my orange hair on top of my head, and told her I was there to put in a formal complaint about Sister Smith. I told her she had just accused me of stealing a patient's walking stick, which obviously was ridiculous, because I had no need for such a thing. And, that for the past week, Sister Smith had been making insinuating and derogatory remarks about me, that were totally unrelated to my work and my training. I didn't have to say more, with Sister

Smiths well known attitude and hatred towards Americans, and that most of the Americans dated girls that were bleached blondes, or prostitute looking women. It didn't matter that I didn't date them, just looking like I did was enough to set her off. Matron told me to calm down, and asked me what my schedule was for the day. I told her I was off until 2 pm. She said to go back to the nurse's home and rest, and everything would be alright when I returned to the ward.

When I got back, Sister Smith had gone off duty for her half day off, and her day off the next day. I was not looking forward to the following day. The other students said that Sister left the floor not long after I had, and that when she returned, she spent most of the morning in her office before she went off duty. I was scared, but it was too late. I couldn't take it back, and deep down I knew I had done the right thing.

When Sister returned, she could not have been nicer to me if she tried. She just about took me under her wing, and proceeded to teach me even more than I ever expected from anyone. She was the sister in charge and I was the student, but the attitude was totally different. I had Mum dye my hair brown, so I did not have to suffer the growing out stage.

Towards the end of my time on D-Ward, Sister said to me: "You like to arrange flowers don't you?" I told her I did, so she told me to do the arrangements for the centre tables. Then one day, she asked me if I would like to try the table at the entrance to the ward. Of course I said I would. She told me to go out into the field next to the ward, and get some branches from the hedgerow to use in it. While I was doing it, Sister Andrew-Arthur, the Sister from C-Ward, came across to see what I was doing. She asked if Sister Smith knew that I was doing it. I told her that it was she who asked me to do it. She just said "Oh!" smiled, and walked away. The next week was to be my last week on the ward. I was asked to do it again. This time I went a bit overboard with my hedge branches, and they stuck out beyond the table. The overall arrangement turned out to be quite stunning, but because of the size I told Sister I would change it. She told me to leave it alone, we would just move the table if it were in the way for the trolleys and stretchers.

I always had a lot of respect for Sister Smith. In that day and time, she could have made my life a living hell for reporting her, which would have been the norm. Instead she turned it around, and taught me not just good nursing skills, but how to treat a subordinate with respect and dignity, and not hold it against me. I wondered if it was because I stood up for myself, when I thought I was right. I decided that was part of it too. From that time on, I decided I would stand up for what I believed was right, for me, or for anyone else that I felt needed or deserved it. As you will find out, that has caused me considerable heartache and difficulties over the years; but I still do it.

It was during this time, that the Rehab Hospital where Dad worked closed down, for the lack of head injury patients needing rehab. Mum and Dad decided to move back to Aynhoe, to buy a piece of land from Auntie Adelaide and build a bungalow on it. Mum, June and Norman, moved in with Gran and Denis, along with some of her furniture.

Mum was doing hairdressing at Gran's again, and travelling to different villages, doing hairdressing in peoples homes. She had bought herself a car and learned to drive. When the house was finally ready to move into, Denis and I moved the furniture in for her, during one of the days she was hairdressing in another village. By the time she returned all was moved in and put away. She just needed to move things, if she wanted them different to where we had put them. Curtains were hung, linen put up, dishes and pots and pans put away. She was very grateful for all we had accomplished.

Some time later, Dad moved in with them. Norman had his own room, June and I shared a room with twin beds, and of course Mum and Dad had their room. Obviously, I only used our room on my days off and during vacations. The bungalow is very nice. There is a large living room, with lots of picture windows, and a large kitchen dining room combination. The centre hallway is large and "L" shaped. Mum turned it into a saloon initially to do her hairdressing.

Dad had got himself a job, driving sports cars to the docks, which were destined to be shipped to the United States. The reason they hired people to do this, was to give the cars a chance to be run-in at a certain speed, prior to going to the States. This was better for the engines, and the reason they didn't go to the States until they were run-in, was because the Americans wouldn't drive them at the required lower speed, for the required 100 miles. I am not 100% sure the British drivers did either, but the thought was there. Dad did this job in all weathers, until he retired at 62 years old. He seemed to enjoy it. He said it was just him and the car and whoever he met on his way back to pick up another car.

June was working in Oxford at the time, as a window dresser in one of the large department stores, and she travelled back and forth each day. Norman was still in school, and went to Banbury Tech School until he finished school. I believe his first job was a beer taster at one of the local breweries. He later joined the Metropolitan Police Force, and worked his way up to the mounted branch.

The garden of the bungalow, had a lot of potential, and Mum and Dad really developed a very pretty garden.

Artist drawing of the Horton General Hospital

The original plans of the Horton

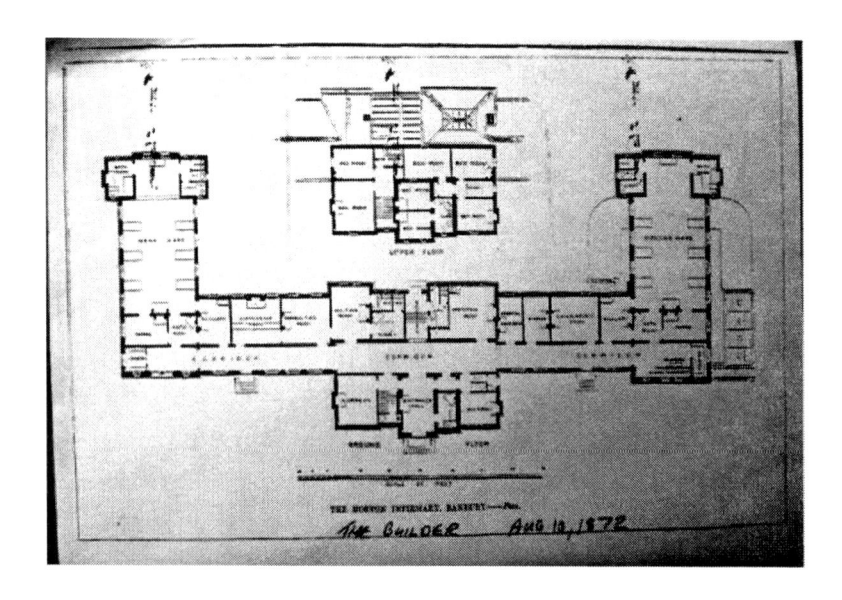

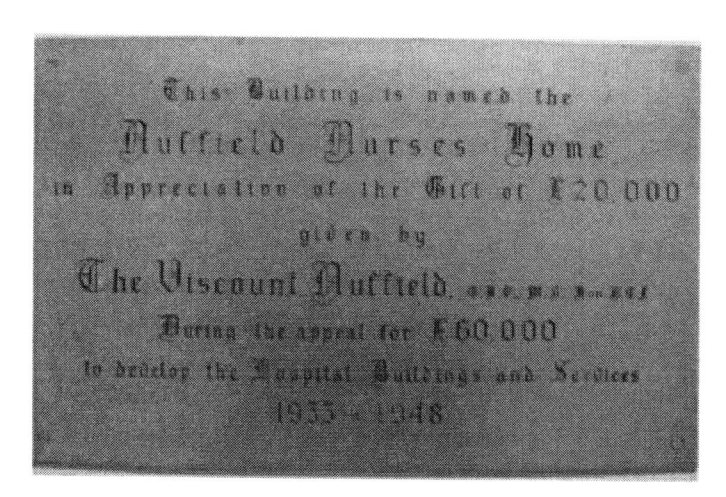

The brass plaque for the
Nurses Home, above

Right: The front garden
of the Nurses Home,
circa 1920

Below: Nurses visitor
sitting room, 1950's

61

Rt. A Ward
At the Horton
1920's

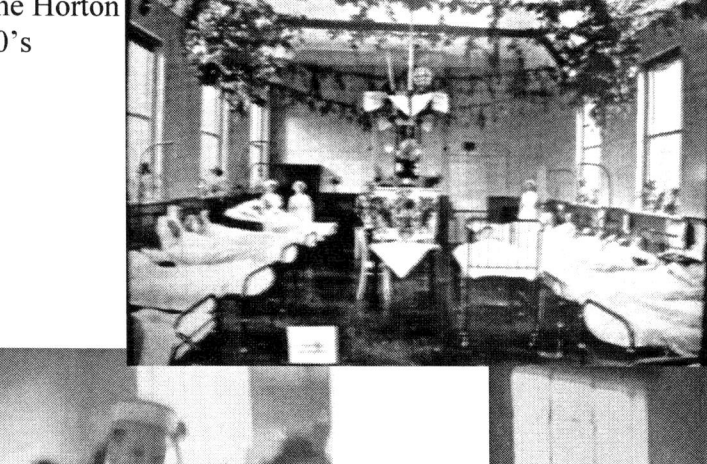

Above: 1947 C-Ward, serving Xmas dinner Dr Wharton and Sister Andrew-Arthur.
Above Rt: 1947 D-Ward Sister Smyth, and Dr Sevitt Serving Xmas dinner

Rt: L-R Nurse Lovell, Dr Sevitt, Dr Wharton, Sister Andrew -Arthur, Sister Donnelly

Left: Holbech Ward 1958: L-R Staff Nurse Vera Clifton, Miss Harvey Assist Matron, Sister Donnelly, Nurse Jennifer Humphris, Father Christmas, Mrs Alford, Matron, Sister Stewart, 2 nurses unknown, Staff Nurse Peggy Tombs

Rt: Holbech Ward 1958: R-L Nurse John Caras-Altus, Staff Nurse Vera Clifton, Dr. Pickering, Sister Stewart, Nurses Margaret Hammer, Jean Paxton, Cynthia Holowell

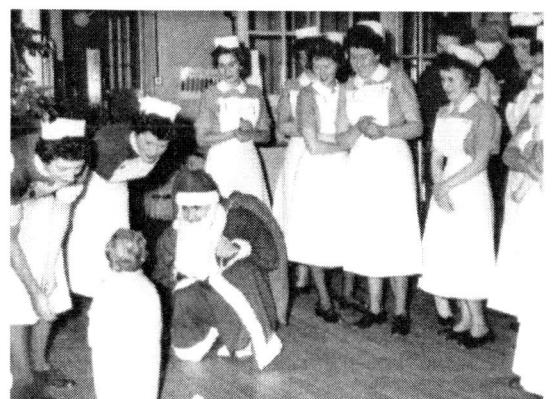

Above Holbech Ward 1958 R-L Staff Nurse Vera Clifton, Sister Donnelly, Father Christmas, 7 first year student nurses, 2nd from Rt Staff Nurse Peggy Tombs

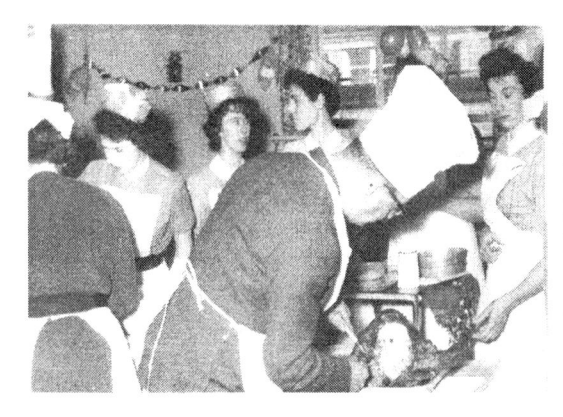

1959 B-Ward serving Xmas Dinner:
L-R Sister Cook, Staff Nurse Lynott, Nurse Pat Ward, Dr. Briggs, Nurse Alison White

Right: Christmas 1955-56 circa.
Ward unknown, 5th from left Nurse Vera White Ward A
L to R Gloria Jarvis
Dr Paddy O'Neil ANNE LEACH
Mr Williams

Left: Prize giving 1962
L-R Miss Day Sister Tutor, Miss Warren, Staff Nurse Alison White, Miss Bourne, Matron

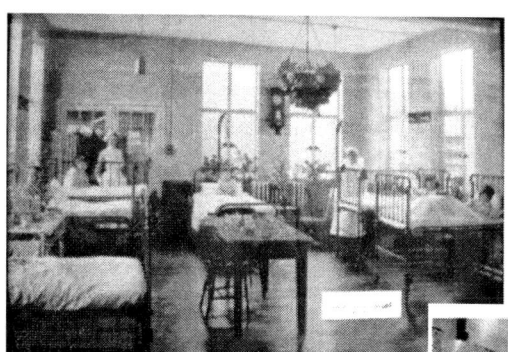

1920's Left Holbech Ward
Below Children's ward
Below Left: Holbech Ward
Far below Right: Women's
Surgical Ward

Children's Ward

Women's Surgical Ward

Left and Below: Patients outside the wards for fresh air and a change of scenery

Left 1920's a celebration outside the old main entrance. Below: Horton gymnasium in the 1920's

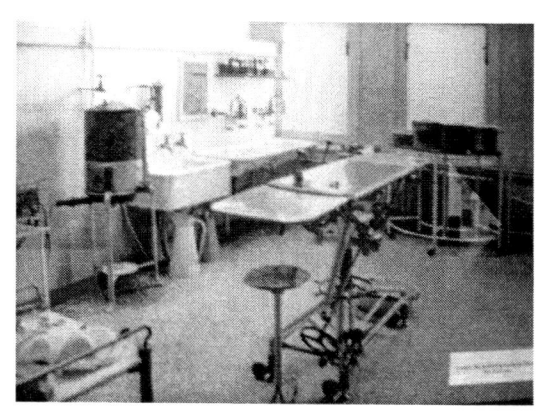

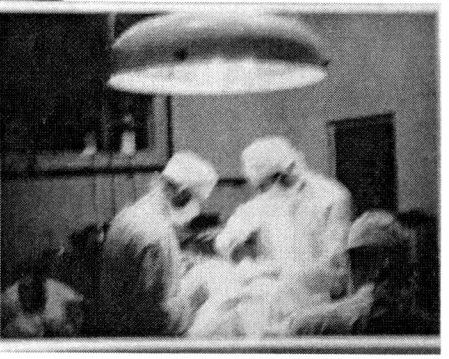

Top, Old small theatre 1920's

Above: Mr. Bardin, Dr Sevitt 1947

Above Right: Mr Bardin, Dr. Sevitt operating Anaesthesia Dr. Glazier 1947

Right: Theatre Sister 1924 Edith M L Smith (Bolton) mother of Christine Bolton

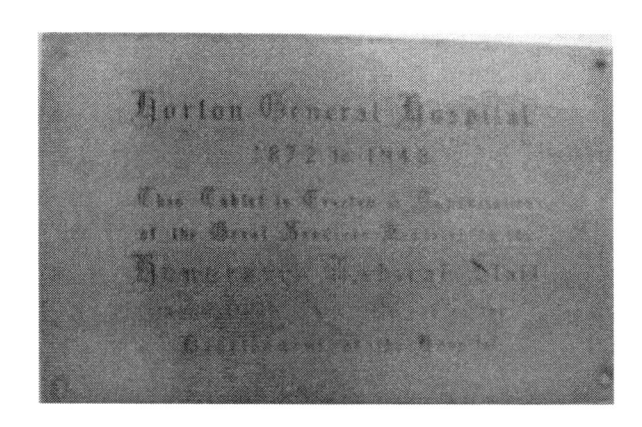

Various brass plaques.
Above left is Penrose House
the Sisters living quarters

Left: Anne Johnson and Dawn Alsford on holiday in 1958.
Below: Anne ? And Dawn on one of our trips to London

Left: John Burden and Anne Johnson out beside the side of the nurses home.
Below: same area, L-R Anne Johnson, Dawn Alsford, Jeanette Boyce

Above right & left:
Graduation groups date unknown
Below; She Cared do You? From the Horton archives

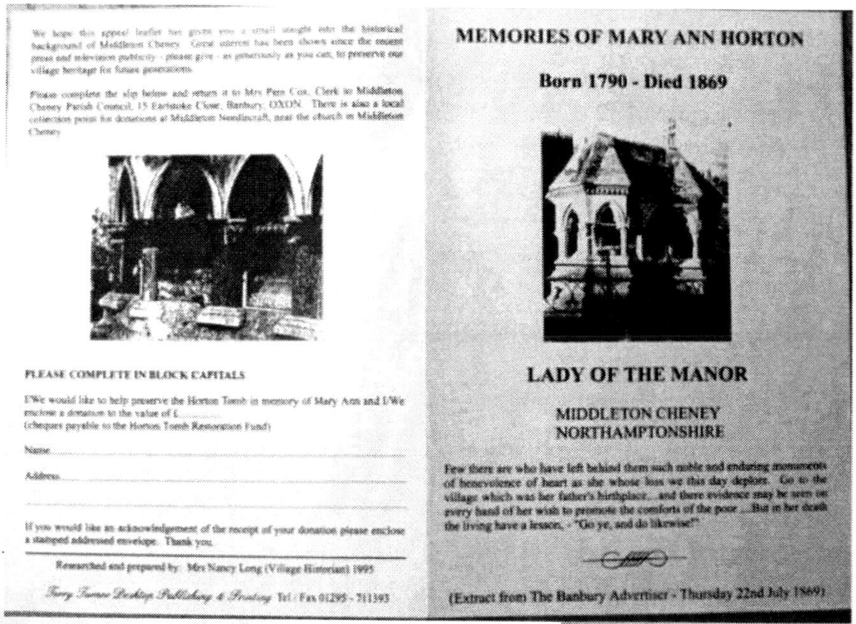

Right and Left: 3rd year students from the 1950's
Below: Margaret McCluskey as a 1st year student

Barbara

Above: Back row, L-R Jennifer Austin, Younger Lynott twin, Pat Ward, Alison White, Front row L-R Jean Ellis, ? Trotman, Pam Cummings, Elaine Buswell.
Above Right: 3 on night duty.
Right: March 1958 starting class, L-R Dorothy Hart, Christine Bolton , Dawn Alsford, Jeanette Boyce

Right: Fancy dress 1959, 4th from Rt Matron, Mrs Alford on the stretcher Christine Bolton

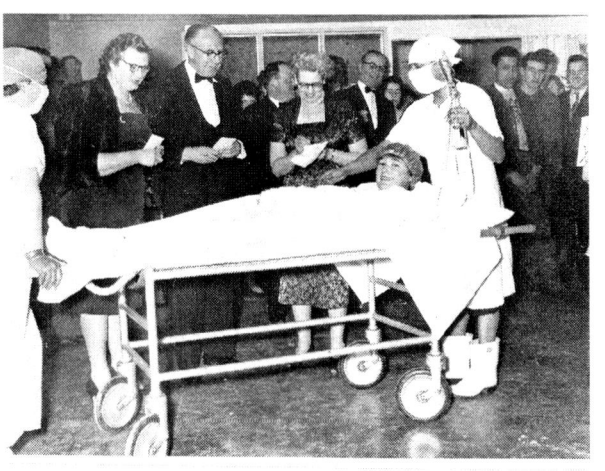

Left: Variety group:1960 of student nurses
Below: Nurses at a Christmas dance at the Crown 1960-61 L-R John England, Alison White, Elaine Buswell, John ?, Lilian Pyrah, Cynthia Hollowell, Peggy Tombs

Above: 15th July 1961 Christine Bolton and David Lunn's wedding.
Right: Guests, Mary Douglas, Dawn Alsford, Dorothy Hart, Doreen Gibbard, unknown

Above: Graduation and prize winners of 1961, front sitting unknown, Doreen Pickersgill, unknown, Jennifer Humphris. Lilian Fisher, Back row L-R Christine Bolton, Miss Day sister tutor, Pat Ward, unknown Lynott twin, Julie Turner, Brennon Twin, John Burns, Dorothy Hart, unknown, unknown, Anne Johnson, Maureen R? Dawn Alsford, Miss Bourne, Matron.

Prize Winners 1960: Back Row L-R Marjorie Harris, Mrs Friswell, Mrs Cheney, Matron Alford, Sir George Schuster, Dr. Jennings, Miss Harvey, Assist. Matron, Brennan twin, Margaret ? Mr. Friswell, Miss Day Sister Tutor, Elaine Buswell.
Middle row, L-R Marie Stirling, Jeanette Boyce, Jean Paxton, Margaret Hammer, Pat Archer, Sheila Tibbetts, Brenda Culf, ? Davies
Front row, John Carrus-Altus, Alison White, Josie Brennan, Jennifer Humphris, Margaret Lyford, Cynthia Millington, John England

Dawn's 21st birthday party: Top lt cake, Top rt Dawn and Anne Johnson, Family group L-R Dad, Syd Alsford, Dawn, Pete Wallace, Mrs. Wallace, Mum Norah Alsford, Norman Alsford, June Alsford, John Carrus-Altus, Len Mowatt. Next right, Maurice Parrish, Ada Parrish (Gran), Gwen Parrish, Eileen Evans. Above left, all the villagers at party having fun. Above right Ada Parrish (Gran) Pat Parrish. Left. Mr. Smart

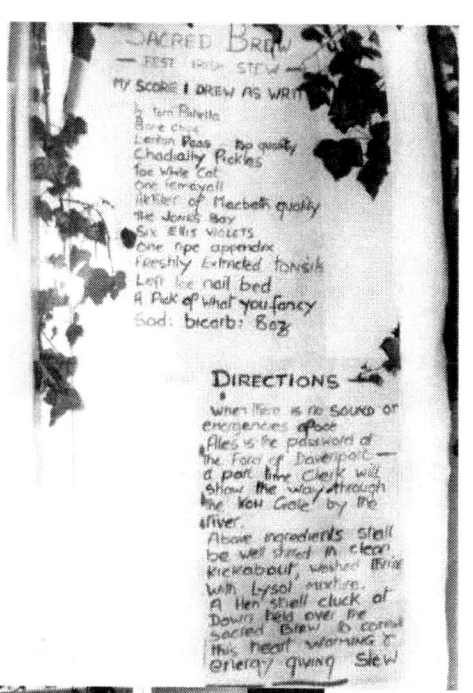

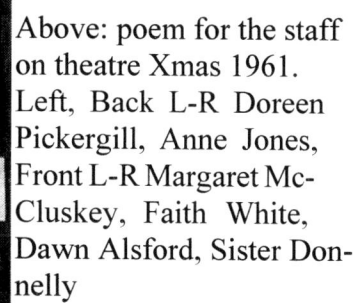

Above: poem for the staff on theatre Xmas 1961. Left, Back L-R Doreen Pickergill, Anne Jones, Front L-R Margaret McCluskey, Faith White, Dawn Alsford, Sister Donnelly

7 th July 1962
Dawn and Mike's wedding
Right L-R Angela, Hilary Barber, Dawn, Norman, June Alsford, Sue Parrish
Below: after the wedding

Some of the Horton Christmas decoration 2006

Chapter 6

Later Student Years

As I progressed further into my second year as a student nurse, the responsibilities increased, as did the lectures and studying requirements. The cleaning became much less, not that I minded. I felt like I had spent most of my life cleaning.

October through December 1959, I worked on the gynaecological, Norris Ward. Sister Regan was in charge there. She was Irish and an ardent Catholic. If any Nuns needed hospitalisation, no matter what was wrong with them, they were put in a private room on her ward. She would fuss over them constantly. We were not permitted to give them any personal care. There was always another Nun in the room, to attend to their every need.

This ward was rarely full, so it was a much more relaxed atmosphere, allowing us more time to do special treats for the patients. We always made the teatime meal for the patients on each ward. Generally speaking, this comprised of a variety of sandwiches, biscuits, scones and cakes. The baked goods came from the main kitchen, the rest we made. On Norris ward, we would make things like Welsh rarebit, eggs in a nest, boiled eggs with bread fingers, or poached eggs on toast.

There were set days for the gynaecological surgeries, so the routine was not stressful at all. The ward was much smaller; only about twenty beds. This allowed us time to do some studying as well. Sister Regan was the kind that, if the work was done, she did not expect you to look busy, or do "busy work". She would much rather you spent time with the patients.

January to April 1960, I was assigned to the outpatient department. This was where clinics were held, for the Horton and Oxford doctors, to see the patients that had been previously admitted to the hospital, or the ones that were going to need admissions. I found the Oxford doctors, for the most part, were much less patient or kind to the patients. The Orthopaedic doctors were the worse!

I remember this one elderly gentleman that had severe arthritis of the spine. He was having an especially hard time, managing to lie flat on the examining table. I was trying to help him, by guiding his legs down the table to stretch them out. This Orthopaedist came in, pushed me to one side, and put one of his hands on the patients' knees, the other on his chest and pushed him down flat. The man screamed in pain. I was so angry with the

MD, that I got between him and the patient, told him he was cruel; that what he did was uncalled for, and I hoped I'd have the chance to do the same thing to him one day. I got reported for that outburst and the usual trouble for being disrespectful. I still think I was right!

One of the top surgeons for the orthopaedics that came down from Oxford, had a reputation of trying to sexually touch the nurses, if he caught one in an examination room alone. He would try and trap you against a wall, push his body against you, and grope you wherever he could. He was middle aged and short. We were told never to go into an examination room on our own, even with a patient in there, and always to take another nurse with us. If he still tried anything, we were to use whatever means necessary, to get him away from us. I had gone into a room one time to get some supplies; it wasn't even in the section he was working in. The next thing I knew he was there, and he had me pinned up against the door so I couldn't escape. So I just kneed him as hard as I could. He really should have been fired.

Outpatients had one very nice bonus, in as much that the physician's regular workweek, other than emergencies, is Monday to Friday, so this meant we had weekends off. We had to work Saturday mornings, during which time we thoroughly cleaned the whole area, and stocked all the rooms. During the week, we worked each day from 7:30 am to 6:00 pm. Having every evening and weekend off was pure luxury.

With the approach of the completion of my second year in training, and getting my second stripe, I was destined for my second stint of night duty. At this level, on nights, we were in charge of the ward we were assigned to. This included all the medication administration, more involved treatments, patient record keeping, and the supervision and teaching of the junior nursing student. We were also responsible for the orderlies and SEAN, (State Enrolled Assistant Nurses) assigned to the ward during the shift. Later they were called SEN, (the Assistant was removed). With the narcotic medications, the night sister came to observe the administration, and to co-sign all the legal records required by law. As it is today, this can only be done by a licensed nurse.

These 12 weeks of nights, I was assigned to A-Ward and B-Ward. The division was about equal. I can't say I liked the men's medical ward, much better than the women's medical ward. But at least on nights I didn't have the ward cleaning to do, and being in charge of the ward and having some say on how things are done, is better than being the lowest person on the totem pole.

The orderly that worked on B-Ward, was a Mrs. Wallace. She was a good worker and very knowledgeable. We got along very well. One night, when we were sitting doing our paperwork, she mentioned she had a son stationed with the RAF in Singapore. He was in the bomb disposal squadron. She asked me if I would be interested in writing to him, while he was over there. She said it was difficult for them being away for so long. He was due back in July, so it wouldn't be for too long. I agreed, if he wanted me to, but he'd have to write first.

We corresponded pretty regularly until he returned home; he asked if we could at least meet after he got home. Pete and I hit it off well from the start, and so started a relationship of almost a year and a half. He was stationed in Whitby Yorkshire. Apparently there were a lot of unexploded bombs from the war, still scattered all over the Yorkshire moors, that needed disarming. There continued to be a lot of letter writing still, but we had decided that after I graduated, and I had finished my post-graduate work, we would get married. In the meantime we would both save, and started a joint savings account at one of the banks in Banbury. At my 21st birthday party I would ask for household items such as linens and things. We were both very organized about it all. He would have time off for my twenty-first birthday party celebration, and he would bring his friend down with him, who would be his best man. I will cover the rest of that story later on. Right now, back to nights and the medical wards.

As usual both wards were very busy, though at least there weren't beds up in the middle. It had long been suspected that B-Ward was haunted. Nothing very drastic, but considering the amount of deaths on the ward it was to be expected. What it amounted to was, when we were sitting doing the paperwork in the middle of the ward, with the screens around us so that the light wouldn't disturb the patients, we would hear footsteps approaching the screens. We would look up to see who was there, and find no one. This was an almost nightly occurrence.

We had a lot of student nurses and Interns from India. Most of them are extremely superstitious, and it took very little to spook them. They used to make it worse for themselves, by constantly talking about things that scared them. Most of them did not like touching, or dealing with the dead patients. At night time it was impossible to get an Intern from India to come and pronounce a death. We would do it, and they would just fill out the paperwork; usually the next day.

Nurses in England in those days, had the job of bathing the patient and stuffing all the orifices and/or tying off the penis of the patients that had died. Tying their chins up, after putting the false teeth in their mouths, so the mouths didn't gape open after rigor mortis had set in. Tying their great toes together, to keep their feet together, and put a nametag on one of the great toes. Then we dressed them in a shroud, wrapped them into a sheet mummy style, and took them to the morgue. Our morgue was outside the building. It looked like a chapel, both inside and out, and was surrounded by huge yew trees, with their spooky groaning sounds.

The first time I laid someone out, was on C-Ward. I didn't think I would ever feel clean again. I had 3 baths, changed all my clothes and washed my hair. I still felt dirty, and as for my nursing scissors - I boiled those for so long, they could have been used on major surgery. It doesn't take very long, and with so many deaths, it becomes as mundane as the most routine job we ever had to do. The only thing we did do, in reality was a form of resuscitation, but we didn't know anything about resuscitation in those days. Let me set the stage: If a patient died on our shift we had to stay behind to lay them out. Now, if everything went straightforward, it took an hour to complete the job. Generally it was an hour and a half. After a twelve hour shift, another one to one and half-hours is not very appealing. We figured that what we did was not going to make any difference to the patient, but it meant a world of difference to us. We found, especially on nights, if we waited to do the AM care on the dying patients, until just before we were due to go off duty, then be especially gentle with them, this after giving them a few good whiffs of oxygen before starting and finishing their care, it would get us out of the door before they died. We would watch them very closely, and if they stopped breathing, which sometimes happened with just two minutes left on duty, we would put the oxygen mask on them, and push the volume up to 10 and down to the bottom again. If we did this three or four times, they would start breathing again and we would be home free. When we came back on duty that night, we would hear it from the other nurses, but they would do the same to us when they had the chance.

This one night on B-Ward, I had a first year student nurse from India working with me. She was known to be not very work brittle. She had come from a wealthy family with servants, so she felt most of what we had to do was beneath her. Her speed was between dead slow and stop! She was very scared to be working on B-Ward, with the reported ghost; she wouldn't stop talking about it.

This particular night we had three or four patients that were close to dying. The first one to die was particularly sad. Her husband had died on

A-Ward just a few nights before. Mrs. Wallace had gone on her dinner break, so I told this nurse we would go ahead and start laying her out, while she was gone, then we would be almost ready to take her to the morgue when she got back. The student wouldn't let it rest, that it was scary that her husband had just died.

We had got along pretty far with all we had to do. She was bathed, stuffed, and I was just trying to get her false teeth in place, when they got hooked up on each other in the back. So I was pretty low down over her, trying to see what I was doing in the limited light, when all of a sudden the patient sat bolt upright in the bed. I saw the student nurse flash by me out of the corner of my eye. I think she cleared the bed in one step. I didn't see her again for the rest of the night. My immediate reaction was; "My God she isn't dead and I've got her all stuffed up." So I am trying frantically to get all the cotton out of the back of her throat and nose. After I got all those out, I tried talking to her, and got no response; just this blank stare straight ahead. By this time Mrs. Wallace had come back, so I asked her to watch her while I went to call the doctor. The doctor refused to come down, (she was Indian also). Instead, she said she is probably dead. Just wait until she goes cold, and then finish laying her out. We do not like waiting until they are cold to lay them out. It is not a pleasant sensation. I called sister and told her what had happened. She did come by and take a look, but didn't offer any other solution. She put out a search for my missing student, without any luck.

When the patient was cold, I tried to lay her down flat, to finish laying her out, and when I put her back down her legs went up in the air. I called sister. She said; get the porter to deal with it. He came down and just put his hands on her legs and chest and pushed. The sound wasn't too pleasant but she was flat. I finished what I was doing. When it was time to take her to the morgue, no-one, not even the porter, would come with me. I ran her to the morgue very fast, pushed her into the first set of doors and left her there on the stretcher. I felt like I had more than done my bit, and that someone else could deal with her in the morning. The student nurse never worked again. It was more than she could deal with.

July through October 1960, I was assigned to the Emergency Room. The staffing here was different from everywhere else. There were two sisters. The head one Sister Crewe was as hard as nails, and very unfriendly towards everyone. The junior sister was very sweet, friendly and kind to all she came in contact with. She was very grandmotherly. She, like all the sisters though, was unmarried and lived in the Sisters Home across the street from the hospital. There was also a senior and a junior staff nurse, and usually three student nurses, all either third year students or, like myself, senior second year students.

The ER had one small operating theatre, a large trauma room, a cast room for setting bones and casting etc. and four treatment rooms. The ER had been renovated before I started at the Horton, so it was the newest addition.

Because this was a farming community, we did receive a lot of farm related accidents, along with the car and motor bike accidents. The latter were most usually the fatal or the more serious injuries. After one week of working in an ER, no-one would get on a motor bike or motor scooter without wearing a crash helmet. Heads, walls, and posts don't mix. The head is always going to come out the loser.

Then, of course, we had the home-related accidents and sports accidents. On Rugby match weekends, we always had extra staff on, to deal with the injuries. The most common being dislocated shoulders. We did not get just sick people using the ER. Mainly because, if someone was sick they would call their doctor to do a home visit. We would only get those, if the doctor determined an admission was necessary, and then they would come in via ambulance.

It was an interesting department to work in; usually feast or famine. This was where I first came into more direct contact with the American GI's. They seemed very susceptible to car accidents, usually from drinking and driving. I think a big contributor was, that at 18 they were legally old enough to drink in England, and that at home they weren't allowed to drink until they were 21. The other reason was; they had never been taught to drink responsibly.

We used to think they were strange, because they insisted on calling the student nurse's 'sergeant' or 'corporal' instead of nurse, because of the stripes on our dress sleeves. We tried to explain it to them, but they didn't listen, and insisted on doing it their way. Doesn't that sound like an American? Their way is the only way - they think!

Remember back in 1956, when I couldn't wait to work in the operating theatre? In October 1960, my dream finally became a reality, and I was going to be allowed to spend more than the usual 3 months there. The reason for this was, that by 1960 medicine was changing rapidly. With the advent of more and more disposable equipment - syringes, needles, IV sets, even some instruments, plus urine testing dip sticks - it decreased the workload for the nurses. It also increased safety for the patients. The proposed development of study blocks for nurses, and the unbelievable 2 days off a week (if the nurse was not needed), these changes were making life much easier on nurses, and student nurses in particular. There were new antibiotics available, along with the development of many new drugs that were saving lives. Along with new surgical procedures and treatments, it was a very revolutionary time.

 I gather that, because of these changes, and because in England they tend to specialize in many different fields of medicine as do physicians, we nurses were allowed to spend more of our last year of training, in the area we intended to specialize in. That is if the hospital could offer it, and we had met all our training requirements. The other requirement in England's nurses, was at the end of formal training, we could not just leave the hospital, and go to work as an SRN in another hospital. We could leave, if we were going to continue our education, at another training hospital, that offered the specialty that we needed. A few examples are; a midwifery school for those wanting to be midwives, Great Ormond Street Hospital for those specializing in paediatrics, and either a psychiatric or orthopaedic hospital, for those interested in those specialties. There were specialties in all fields. If a nurse did not want to do a specialty, then she was required to stay at the hospital that she trained at, to do essentially a year internship as a junior staff nurse. With that completed, the nurse could either stay on in a senior capacity, if there was an opening, or find work in another hospital. It wasn't uncommon for nurses, at this point, to start travelling throughout the commonwealth. It could be a wonderful experience. My plan was to go to Nigeria, then New Zealand and Australia, after I had done my years post-graduate in the Operating Theatre. I did think I might do year psychiatry, just for good measure.

 Operating theatre nursing, is unlike any other within the hospital setting. There is even more camaraderie between all the staff, including the surgeons, than in any other part of a hospital. I found that to be true on both sides of the Atlantic. You have to work together to get anything accomplished, in what could be a very stressful environment. The working hard, and joking during cases, as was portrayed in the TV program Mash, is pretty accurate. One has to do something to keep ones sanity.

 Staffing consisted of Sister Donnolly, a senior, a junior staff nurse, and preferably 2 or 3 junior ones, especially if the student nurses are inexperienced in surgery. Student nurses varied in numbers from 1 to 4, all being third year students or very close to third year. There was the most valuable porter, who did all the very heavy lifting for us, and ran the autoclaves for the linens. He taught the student nurses, who were new to the theatre, how to operate the autoclaves. We had to know this, in case we needed to run one in the middle of the night, when we had an emergency surgery and needed more linen.

Obviously the staff nurses taught the new student, as did the student that had more experience. We were constantly learning, because there were always new things coming out. The idea was to have all members of the staff, including all the students, to be competent enough to take nighttime and weekend call, for emergency surgeries. There were always two nurses on call at a time. One that was qualified to scrub in, to pass instruments etc. to the surgeons; the circulating nurse's job, is to pass anything that is needed to the table, and to hang the soiled swabs for counting. This is to guarantee none are left inside a patient. I am not going to explain all the technicalities of the different surgeries, but rather the background operations that were done in those days, before such conveniences as central supply and surgical pack.

Theatre was a domain all unto itself. There were the changing rooms for men and for women, generally considered the nurses and the doctors' rooms. Although, with the advent of more male nurses and female doctors, the names were changed. Sister had her office next to the autoclave room, and the women's changing room was next to her office. There was a large open area, where work such as packing drums for autoclaving, patching gloves prior to sterilizing, counting and stocking supplies was done. There were large storage cupboards, and trolleys were kept there, that were used to transport patients back and forth from the wards to surgery. Sometimes it was a holding area for patients as well.

Off of this area were the entrances to the anaesthesia room, where patients were put under, with a door directly from there into the operating theatre. There was also an entrance to the theatre from the main open area. From this area, there was an entrance to the scrubbing area, for the surgeons and nurses to scrub prior to going into surgery. So, of course, there was a direct entrance from there into the theatre. There was also a pass way through to the area where the instruments, pans and carts, were cleaned and sterilized following surgery. At the back of this room was the clean area, where the sterile trolleys were made up, in preparation for the day's surgery schedule. What separated these areas, were two huge sterilizers. Each was identical. One was used for a week while the other rested. The sterilizers were heated with gas, and each had a large and a smaller side. The large size was about three feet square, three feet deep and filled with water. All of the pans, trays or bowls, that were going to be needed for any given surgery, were placed in this to be sterilized. This was accomplished by bringing the water to the boil, and maintaining the boiling temperature for a minimum of twenty minutes. They were removed using sterile cheetals, to pick them up without contaminating them, and placed on a sterile surface on the cart used for the instruments. The carts were made sterile, by using the autoclaved linens to drape over each cart. The smaller sterilizer, that was part of the same unit, was heated the same way, and again used water as the medium. This sterilizer was about fifteen inches wide in the front and back, and three feet long and deep. Large metal trays, with holes in the bottoms and sides, were made to fit in it, allowing enough room to bring them out, again using cheetals to maintain sterility. In those trays were placed all the instruments, that it was anticipated would be used for a particular surgery. So, if six surgeries were planned for the day, there would be six trays of instruments. As these were taken out of the sterilizer, they were arranged on each trolley in very specific order, so that the scrub nurse knew where every instrument was, without having to look at it. This was frequently very necessary, if she was helping the surgeon by holding an instrument or retractor in place, and had to reach back for another instrument, without being able to actually look at the trolley.

There was always the same number of instruments used for each specific case, and this had to be learned and memorized. The scrub nurse, with the circulating nurse, is responsible for the counting of all swabs, sponges and instruments, before and after each case; or rather before the surgical sight is closed. The circulating nurse counts along with the scrub nurse, and all is recorded. After all the trolleys are prepared for the day, then they are covered with the sterile drapes to await their turn for use. There was an entrance from this section directly into the theatre, and an entrance from the dirty side into the theatre. Dirty stuff is never taken through the clean section. The dirty section had two very large deep sinks for clean up after each case. At the end of each days operating schedule, everything is taken out of the theatre, and the walls and floors are scrubbed with disinfectant. All of the furnishing got the same treatment, prior to being moved back in. At the end of the day everything sparkled. Of course the anaesthesia room, the scrubbing room, the clean room and lastly the dirty room, all got the same treatment. The porter cleaned the men's changing room, and we did the women's.

The only exception to this routine, was if orthopaedic cases had to be done in the afternoon, following any other type of surgery. Then the theatre had to be scrubbed down before it could be started. The reason for this is, that bones are so susceptible to infection, that it is necessary to take every possible precaution, to prevent any infection in them. Naturally we tried very hard, to keep all orthopaedic cases in one day from start to finish, but emergencies have to be dealt with. Having only one operating theatre, in such a busy hospital, was a problem.

The Operating theatre was exempt from the weekly big cleaning as done on the wards. The only difference was that we did it on the weekends. Saturdays we did all the wheels on all the furnishings. The only difference was we took the wheels off to scrub and oil them. The operating table was jacked up so we could clean its wheels. The other thing we did on Saturdays, was to wash all the ceilings, which meant emptying each room of furniture to do it.

Why were we so particular about the wheels throughout our training? That is easy to explain, if one thinks about a hospital function. People come in very ill or injured. During those times people bleed, vomit, urinate and defecate, not always in the best places. Most usually, at least part of any of the above ends up on the floor. Almost every piece of equipment in a hospital has wheels on it, and try as one might to clean things up when they happen, the patients emergency needs takes precedence. Therefore wheels go through not such clean stuff, and can be trackedanywhere in the hospital. We were taught, that wheels and floors were the biggest cause of cross contamination and infection. It was imperative to counteract it in the best way possible,

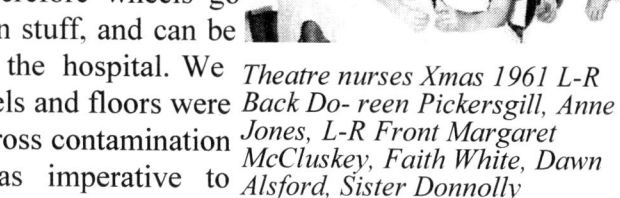

Theatre nurses Xmas 1961 L-R Back Do- reen Pickersgill, Anne Jones, L-R Front Margaret McCluskey, Faith White, Dawn Alsford, Sister Donnolly

and that we knew how. That was the reason for the stringent wheel and floor cleaning. I am certain that is why we did not have the awful bugs that are around today.

I am not saying student nurses need to go back to the way it was in my day, but the people doing the cleaning should be educated, and taught how important it is to clean, and how to clean properly, not taking short cuts. Many I have found are so poorly educated, and with limited intelligence, that they are often not capable of learning, or understanding the reasons for the need for cleanliness. The type of people we need for these positions, need to understand just how important they and their job are, and paid accordingly. Maybe then we would be able to attract the right people.

Back, to the operating theatre cleaning. Sunday was a more relaxed day. This was the day we oiled all the instruments with 3 in 1 oil, and greased all the blades of instruments that weren't used very often. These were cleaned and re-greased every week. Some I never even saw used in the whole time I worked there, but we still cared for them.

I stayed in the operating theatre until the end of April 1961. Therefore I was proficient enough, to share some of the on-call time, along with the staff nurses. If we were called out, and worked 4 or more hours through the night, we did not have to start work until noon the next day. But less than 4 and we had to be at work by 7:30 am. I have always been one of those people who, throughout my career, seems to attract emergencies. So it was a rare night for me if we didn't have at least one case. It was usually many more.

At the beginning of May 1961, I was due to do my last stint on night duty. In fact, as it happened, all the students from my class were back on nights for the last required time. I was assigned to C-Ward again. This time I was way beyond the shyness and blushing side. And, as third year students, our responsibilities were very similar to the junior staff nurses. We were expected to know how to supervise, teach, and instruct the junior students. By this time, we were expected to have developed our own way of accomplishing this.

What I developed, and have not appreciably changed throughout the years, was relatively simple. Always ask a person to do something: Never just tell them to do it. Never ask a person to do something I would not, or have not, done myself. Never tell a person off in public. Always praise a person as they deserve, for something well done, or something that was done extra. Never "talk down" to a person, or treat them any differently than I would like to be treated. I always tell people working for or with me, that I expect all jobs to be well done and done properly; I will not tolerate slip-shod work. I expect all their work to be done and when it is done. I do not expect them to do "busy work". I will not tolerate unkindness, disrespect or rudeness to anyone, whether it's a patient, family member or co-worker. If you don't know something, or how to do something, ask; do not guess. That is how lives are lost. You cannot be expected to know everything; no one does. If what you are asked to do is beyond your capabilities, say so. No-one should do anything they are not capable of doing; again that could cause a loss of life. One mistake or error in working,

I will tell, correct, or show you the right way; the second time, for the same thing you are going to be reprimanded. Finally, always thank whoever has worked with you, or for you, during the shift, a little appreciation goes along way.

      Some students then, and co-workers since, have thought of me as a "real task master", but they have also said they knew where they stood with me. I was fair, and when necessary I would work right along with them, no matter what the job was. And at the end of the day they knew they were appreciated, and that I would stand up for them when necessary. They also have liked the fact, that I will fight for the patients through to the bitter end. In the States, the hospital administrators (head of the hospital) and doctors, didn't like that side of me. I say tough!

      This time on C-Ward was a fun time for me; maybe because I was more comfortable in what knowledge I had, and how to use it. Though, one has to remind oneself, as our Sister Tutor Miss Day used to tell us: "When you think you know everything - you know nothing. When you think you know so little - you are beginning to know something."

      There was one incident that happened on the ward, that I still chuckle about. We had a patient in the ward that was under constant police guard. He had murdered his wife, and then tried to slit his own throat without success. He underwent surgery to repair what he had done, and expected to be hospitalised for about a week. At night time on this ward, we put the screens up around our work area, against the private room wall, because all the more critical patients were kept in that area. The prisoner was in that area, along with one very elderly gentleman that was a bit disoriented from the anaesthesia; this is relatively common in the elderly. The policeman was sitting with his back to the screen, reading a newspaper. The rest of us were either at the table, or sitting in an armchair doing paper work.

      All of a sudden we heard a ping, and the bobby said, "Hum, something just hit my paper." He looked around on the floor, but couldn't see anything; the floor was a dark brown colour. This was followed by several more pings, and watching his newspaper we could see it move, but still couldn't see what it was. I went around the other side of the screen. Everything looked normal and all the patients appeared to be sleeping. Then it happened again, 2 - 3 times in quick succession. The decision was that everyone would continue talking as if nothing was going on, and I would go outside the screens and stand in the dark, to see if I could catch what was going on.

The elderly gentleman was taking something off his bedside table and tossing it over the screen. I went quietly to his bedside to see what he was throwing. He had been incontinent of very dark constipated stool, so it looked like little pellets. He had a pile of them on his bedside table, and he was breaking them off and throwing them over the screen. The bobby just about lost it when he found out what it was. We all thought it was hilarious.

I was able to do a fair amount of studying on nights, ready for our finals in June. If we passed our exams, we were back-paid to the time we took the exams at the SRN rate of pay. This would be £40 a month before deductions, instead of the £12 a month that we were currently getting. We would be rich!

The exams came and went, and the results would be out the end of July. As all of us were still on nights, there wasn't going to be anyone to go to the post office to pick up the results. Then I came up with an idea: Trinder's, the local funeral home/taxi/wedding car service. The daughter of the owners was a friend of mine, and I had dated her brother at one time. I would see if they would send a cab to pick them up, and bring them to the hospital at a designated time I would meet them and pay for the taxi. Trinder's said they would be more than happy to do it. I just had to get the OK from the post office. I called the post office, and gave them the sad story about us all working etc. He didn't take any convincing; nurses are very popular group of people in Banbury. So all was set.

The aforementioned night arrived. I had been to see Mum, who was in D-Ward having undergone surgery the day before. She told me I had to come and tell her the results, as soon as we got them. Two o'clock in the morning, all four of us are out front waiting for the taxi. He opened the door and said they are all low postage, so you've all passed. We had to look to make sure. He wouldn't let us pay for the taxi. He said Mr. Trinder had said it was his treat, and the driver said the tip was his treat. We all hugged each other and cried a little. It had been a long hard haul. I went down to D-Ward and told Mum. She told me she would buy my silver belt buckle for my SRN uniform. When I returned to C-Ward, the lights were all on, and everything was set up for a party with refreshments, wine and the works. I said: "What are you doing? You're going to get me in trouble again".

Several of the patients in the ward, were the same patients that were there that first time I worked there, back in the beginning of my training. It was a very pleasant and appropriate coincidence. Apparently they had got permission from night sister to have this for me. They had it hidden all evening, and worked like crazy to have it all ready for when I got back to the ward, from meeting the taxi. The patients had bought the wine, and their families had made all the refreshments. I asked them: "What would you have done if I had failed." They said that wouldn't have happened, but if it had; then it would have been a consolation party. As it turned out, the whole hospital knew what they had planned, and I didn't even have an inkling. It was so very special to me, and really quite unbelievable, though typical of the way Banbury people feel towards their nurses.

I had a two week holiday planned, starting the next day, to help Kath, a friend of the family, do Mum's hairdressing while she was in the hospital. Kath later became my aunt when she married Denis, When I returned, I would be starting my post - graduate course in the theatre.

Mum was going to be out of work for at least two weeks. Kath was also a hairdresser and worked with Mum. She couldn't do it all on her own, not that I was a hairdresser. The decision was, that I would wash the customer's hair, and put the rollers in according to how it was needed. I would put them under the dryer, and when dry, take the rollers out and give them a good brush. Then Kath would do the styling. Kath would do the haircuts, perms, and any dying that needed to be done. As for going to the different villages, to do the schedule hairdressing, I don't think Kath drove at this time, or if she did didn't feel comfortable with it. I had a 125 cc Vespa scooter, and the decision was that we would pack up the stuff, hairdryer and all, and travel that way. Bearing in mind this wasn't a hand held hair dryer. It was one the customer sat under. It did collapse down a bit.

This is what we did for two weeks. We must have been a sight, careering around on this scooter, totally laden down with equipment and supplies. I didn't make any money at it, but Kath and I had lots of laughs and fun doing it. Mum's customers were so grateful, that they didn't have to go without having their hair done, and Mum still had an income while she was in the hospital.

Kath eventually married my Uncle Denis, on 4th July 1964. This was several years after she got a divorce from her first husband. Her two daughters were very attached to Denis from the start. Their last name was the same as Denis', and spelt the same way, so it made things easier for them from the start.

I do not want anyone to get the wrong impression. Life at the Horton was definitely not all work and no play. I mentioned earlier, that the Horton nurses had the reputation of being great nurses, but they also knew how to have fun, and threw some fabulous parties. We worked hard and we played hard. Besides the Wednesday dances at the church house, run by Alf and Pat, my Aunt and Uncle, there was also the Saturday dances at the Winter Gardens. Those dances were usually music from either professional, or semi professional bands. Initially it was the big band sound, then came the era of rock and roll groups, traditional jazz bands, and skiffle groups. The Winter Gardens were part of a pub, so drinks were available too. The only trouble with the Winter Gardens was, when the American GI's came, started flashing their money around, and tried taking the English girls away from their English boyfriends. Some nasty fights broke out. In the end a lot of people stayed away. We said; just let the Yanks have it and we will find somewhere else. Their behaviour was so brash, abrasive, and rude that we preferred their room to their company.

Traditional Jazz Festivals were very popular at this time, especially if they were all night ones. We would hitchhike miles to a festival (that being the normal form of transportation in England at the time). Especially for Acker Bilk, Kenny Ball or Chris Barber, all of which came to the Winter Gardens early on, before the Yanks took over. The all night ones were indoors, usually in large dance halls. There would be several groups scheduled to play, and when they weren't playing they mingled with the dancers. It was all very relaxed and lots of fun.

We used to hitchhike to the Towcester races, especially if we were short of money, as we usually were the week before the end of the month. We would bet on the jockeys rather than the horses. We knew which jockeys only rode good horses, and we would bet at the bookie stands rather than at the tote. We would get our bet in early, when it was still 20 to 1, and just put a shilling on it. When it won, that meant £1 winnings. If we placed bets like that 2 or 3 times, we were more than set until the end of the month. We never bet more than a shilling and never more than 3 times. It worked for us, and kept us in money until payday. Being paid only monthly, it was difficult to make it last the full time. The people in town always knew when our payday was, especially the restaurants and tearooms. We could finally afford to get some decent food. The first place we would hit after payday, was the Grill just below St John's Church. They had the best Mixed Grill I have ever eaten. The price of the meal was 2s6d. It included grilled sausage, lamb chop, steak, tomatoes, mushrooms, peas and chips; it was so good after the hospital food. One month our pay cheque's came through earlier than usual, so we were able to make it to the Grill before they expected us. The owner said something to us about paying for it, that he knew we had no money before payday. We thought he was joking so we talked amongst ourselves, about how many dishes we would have to wash to pay for the meal. When we went up to pay for it he said; we know you don't have any money, so one of the other customers has already paid for you all. We tried to tell him we were joking we got paid earlier than usual and we could pay for it. He said the other customer had already left and he didn't know his name. We all felt awful about it. He told us not to worry: The customer seemed very happy to help us, because he knew we were all nurses. It was not at all unusual for us to go to a tearoom for a meal, only to find someone had paid for it before they had left. But this was different. There was about six of us, and in those days that was a lot of money.

It was about 1960 that Matron offered for all the nurses to have a monthly party in the nurses' home. She would supply us with the party snacks; we were responsible for the drinks and music. Between us we had plenty of records, and the nurses' home had a pretty good record player. So as far as the music was concerned, we were all set. The drinks were another obstacle we had to overcome. We decided for the first one to make a large bowl of hot punch. Hot, because that would mask some of the flavours liable to be in it. For the first one we got a variety of cheap wines, several bottles of regular hard cider, one Merrydown cider, the kind that no-one can supposedly drink one bottle of and stay standing, and some cheap gin. To this we added several bottles of lemonade, (similar to 7-Up), several slices of oranges and lemons, about six slices of toast and two pounds of sugar. We brought this to a boil and let it simmer very gently for about two hours. Then we strained it. Just before the party started, we brought it to the point of being a hot drink, and added fresh slices of fruit. This was served to everyone when they first arrived, and there was enough for everyone to have at least 2-3 glasses. It had a really good flavour, and the fact that the rest of our drinks were not quite top quality, didn't seem to matter. Some of the patients, when they heard we were having a party, contributed some bottles, as different patients continued to do so each month. From that time on, whatever was left from one month, was put into the next months punch, along with whatever we needed to make up the same basic recipe. All our guests thought it was the best punch ever. We never told anyone the ingredients. In reality, they never were the same twice.

The nurses' home had 3 living rooms and one large games room. The games room was used for dancing, and at the entrance to it was where the punch was served. The largest living room was where the snacks and other drinks were; it all worked very well. The only rules Matron had, were that the party had to break up at midnight quietly, so as not to disturb the patients on C- Ward, and that during the evening people were not to take the party outside, which would also have disturbed them.

It was lots of inexpensive fun, for us all and our boyfriends. They especially liked it because it didn't cost them anything, though most of them brought bottles, to either be used that night, or for the future punch. They did not want us to stop making that.

Balls were very common in those days. These of course, were formal affairs. The women all wore evening dresses; some of the men wore tuxedoes, while others just wore dark suits or dress uniforms. Matron had a Ball once a year, and all nurses off duty were expected to attend. It was a grand affair, held in one of the ballrooms in Banbury. The other Balls we were invited to regularly - with the invitations to us coming through Matrons office - were to the various British officers clubs at the military camps around the area. There were several British air force and army camps. Some were quite large and are still around. Others were quite small and were eventually closed down. With these they always sent transportation for us both ways, and again these were full evening dress.

There was one in particular I remember. It was probably late in 1959 to 1960. It was a small RAF camp that we had been invited to several times in the past, but this time it was because it was closing down. We had permission to stay out until 1 am. The next day there was a call to the nurses' home. One of the officers from the camp said the party was still going on, though no longer formal. Were any of us interested in continuing it with them? I had taken the call. I told them I would check around, but most of us were working until 8:30pm. They said they would pick us up and bring us back in the morning. I checked with several of the other nurses, some of them were staff nurses too. Anyway, there were about 6 or 8 of us interested. We told them we had to be back for 5am, so we could get back into the nurse's home without being seen. They said that was no problem. This went on for three nights, and all went well; each of us catching a few hours sleep during our off time during the day. The third night the camp had had all the power shut off, so it was all by lanterns and candlelight. There was still plenty to eat and drink. We all knew this would be the last time we could get together, so we spent most of the time talking. In the morning we decided we would like boiled eggs for breakfast, but the water had been cut off, there was plenty of beer left, so we used that to boil them in, over an open fire. It worked.

When it came time to leave, we were going to have to go back in this broken down vehicle, because the person who had the good one had already gone to another camp. In this one, you could see the road through the floorboards as you sat in the back seat. The only way the doors stayed shut, was after everyone was in the car, you tied rope from one door to the other. This kept them shut. The engine had very little power. Luckily there were only 5 of us that night, but with the two fellows as well, it was pretty well loaded. When we got to this one hill and the car gave out. We still had about 4 miles to go, which turned out to be quite a walk. By the time we all got back to the hospital it was a little after 7 am, and we were due on duty at 7:30. Pickers and I were the only ones that had to get to the nurse's home. The others lived in private digs. We knew if we tried to go through the nurse's home, that Molly would spot us. Picker's was getting very panicky about getting into trouble. I said that maybe if we are so obvious, then we wouldn't be noticed. That if we just walked right through the main part of the hospital, to the nurse's home, we'd get away with it. There was no way Molly would see us then. That's what we did, and thought we had done very well.

At about 9am, I was summoned to Matrons office, with the added information that someone saw me come in. On my way up there, I got prompted by the others not to squeal on them.

Norris Ward Xmas 1961 L-R Mayor of Banbury, ? , Mr Gate, Sister Reagan, Mayoress Banbury,?, ?, Anne Johnson, Margaret Mc- Cluskey, Dawn Alsford

Matron said; I had been seen coming into the hospital just after seven o'clock not dressed for work, and that someone else was with me, but they couldn't see who it was. She asked me where we had been, who the other person was, and if there were any more involved. I told her we had been to a party, at the same place the Ball had been a few nights before; that it was the night before they were all leaving, that the car had broken down, and we had to walk back making us late for curfew. She asked me again who the others were. I told her I couldn't tell her that. She asked me if I expected to be able to work after being up all night. I told her I thought I would be alright. I got off at 6 pm so I would be able to go to bed early. Luckily she didn't know we had been without a nights sleep for the past 4 nights. She told me I would not be any use to the patients, having been up all night, and that I was to go to my room and sleep. I was to report for duty the next morning, and that I could not have a late night pass for the anywhere anyway. I didn't tell her that.

When I got back to the nurses home, the others were down there having a coffee break, and wanted to know what happened. They were relieved I hadn't told on them. Though I think I came off best, because I got to sleep and they all had to work through the day!

There was a student nurse, Anne that had started her training in one of the London hospitals, and because of family problems, transferred to the Horton to finish her training. She had a very different personality from the rest of us. Maybe it was working in London. She was having a difficult time making friends with anyone. We worked together quite a bit, and I found that once you got used to her brash ways, she really was quite nice. Definitely worldlier than the rest of us.

I was very curious about life in general in London. She said she was willing to show me some of the side of London, that most visitors didn't see. Like Petticoat Lane and Soho at night. Petticoat Lane was fascinating. It is an open market in the Cockney part of London. The story goes, that the vendors there will steal your coat off your back at one end of the market, sell it back to you at the other end, and you won't even recognize it. Pickpockets abound there, so you have to be very careful with your handbag. Everything imaginable is sold there, and the vendors all shout against one another, trying to get your custom. Bartering is expected. They shout that the items they have for sale been stolen, but that the previous owners have been paid the insurance, so now everyone is happy. They didn't say anything about how the insurance company felt! They also had people with monkeys, trying to get you to hold them while they take your photo with it, so they can charge you an outlandish price for it.

We went to Soho several different times. There was so much to see there. Coffeehouses were the big rage at the time. One of the famous ones was the "2, I's". One that fascinated me was the "Macabre". This one had coffins for tables', skeletons and cobwebs everywhere; the whole place was painted black with very low lights. It just served coffee with spooky music. There was another place called "Sam Wedges". Anne told me, before we went in there, don't stare at anyone, and don't make conversation with anyone but her. She said it was full of transvestites, and a few other weirdoes. They were all quite harmless as long as we gave them their space.

Inside, the tables were wide, and long enough for eight or more people to sit down each side of the table. Seating was a bench. We sat at the first table inside the door. The atmosphere inside was very jovial, and everyone seemed to know each other. The men/women were dressed very well in female clothes. Most had long hair in women's styles, along with makeup and well-manicured nails. The only way one could really tell they were all men, were their elbows. They were very bony. Not rounded and smooth as women's are. Their voices were deep, but not really masculine. Sitting at the table at the back of the room, was an old man dressed as a man, with a baggy tweed suit on, and a big floppy hat that he sometimes wore. Other times it was on the table or bench beside him. His hair was white, long and shaggy, as was his beard. In front of him he had several very thick huge books; they remind you of wizards or witches books. When I stood up, I noticed there were astrological designs on the pages. Different people would go up to him, sit on the bench across the table from him, and they would carry on a long quiet conversation. After we left, Anne told me he was an Astronomer, and an Astrologist. He is always there, and people are just consulting with him. We went back several times. We made ourselves as inconspicuous as we possibly could - no one objected to us being there.

The other instructions I received from Anne, were to keep moving, not to stand still anywhere on the street in Soho, because I could be standing on someone's beat. They each had their designated spots on the street or corners, and if they caught you standing there, they would think you are trying to cash in on their territory. These were prostitutes. I didn't see anyone that looked like a prostitute to me; when I said so to Anne, she said that if they are women, and standing still, they are prostitutes. There was a beautiful girl about 19 year's old leaning against a shop window. She had short dark curly hair and a lovely complexion. She was wearing a purple gingham dress, with a white Peter Pan collar, and the fashionable many petticoats under her dress, along with white stiletto high heals, white gloves and handbag. I said to Anne: "Even her?" Her reply was: "Oh yes." Her face and appearance has stuck with me over the years. It just seemed such a waste, and always made me wonder why.

Soho also had a large variety of restaurants, representing many ethnic backgrounds. We especially liked the Indian Curry, and it is much hotter than the Chinese curry. We always made sure whatever we ordered, we could tell what animal or bird it was made from. Our favourite was whole chicken curry. It was served in a large soup tureen with loads of rice and large jugs of lager. We had the lager because it was served cold, and we needed something to counteract the heat from the curry. It was worth the suffering to get the flavour.

Whenever we went to London, we took the train and then caught the last train back. That would get us into Banbury by 11:40 pm, and then, with the taxi, be back before curfew at Midnight. Of course this was on Saturday nights. One Saturday we missed the last train. We didn't have enough money for a hotel, so we decided the safest place to spend the night, was on one of the benches in St James Park. Anne called an old boyfriend up and explained our predicament. He said he would come and spend the night there with us, and then no-one would bother us. We found some newspapers someone had left behind, and covered ourselves with them. It works. It keeps the cold out. We caught the first train to Banbury the next morning, and we were back at work on time that day. This time I didn't get caught.

Twenty-first birthdays were very big celebrations in those days. I had always said I wanted mine in the village hall, so I could invite the whole village to it. Young and old alike, it was a party dress affair. Hilary Barber and Brian Mullins came down from Oxford. He was the boy she used to sit up front with, at the cinema on Saturdays; they got married a few years later. My cousin Tony, and his parents came down from London, plus his new girlfriend Eileen, who he also married a few years later. Of course Gran and all my other relatives and friends came, including the young and old from the village. Mum and Dad gave me some money towards it. Pete bought the beer. The rest I saved the money to make it possible. We all did a lot of cooking. Jean Oakey baked 80 cream horns. I made the birthday cake, the same type as our Christmas cakes. I made my dress for it; over the years I had made all my clothes. If I hadn't, my wardrobe would have been very skimpy. The day after the party, everyone said it was the best village gathering since before the war.

I had asked anyone that wanted to bring a gift to bring something for a hope chest, because of Pete and my plans. They were all expecting a formal engagement announcement, which was what we had planned. But at the last minute, neither one of us wanted to do that. As the months went by and we realized we really didn't want that commitment. We decided to go our separate ways just before Christmas 1962.

Following the nights on C-Ward and the couple of weeks helping Kath with the hairdressing for Mum, I was scheduled to start my post-graduate course in the theatre.

Chapter 7

Life Changes and Mike

Being an SRN, doing a post-graduate course in the theatre, did not change the cleaning work that needed to be done by all. The only difference really, was the level of responsibility, and not needing a licensed nurse to oversee what you were doing. Outside the theatre we got to wear the staff nurse's uniform, which was a royal blue and fully lined dress with long sleeves, (not good in the summer heat). The starched collar was more comfortable, because it laid flat against your neck instead of gauging it, as our student one did. In the theatre we all wore scrub dresses. They were much more comfortable than the traditional uniforms.

Shortly after I started doing my post-graduate course, we were down to only 2 nurses qualified to scrub up; a senior SRN, Margaret McCluskey, and myself. This meant we were also the only two that could be on call. With that arrangement, one of us was on call 4 nights one week, and three nights the next week. To cover the theatre day and night with this schedule, and because it was a rare night that we did not have at least one emergency case to do, it wasn't long before we began to be a little the worse for wear. We were eating at the same speed we were working, which was at top speed. This caused us to start having severe indigestion problems. I think, in reality, that they were more concerned that we would get sick, and not be able to work, than for our well-being. We were examined by the nurses MD a Dr. Anne Davis, who said the problem was, that we were so wound up, from the speed we were working, that we were not digesting our food properly. If we were not given a chance to slow down we would be out of work. Her solution was - we were to be allowed enough time before eating, to go to the nurses' home, sit down and smoke at least half a cigarette to calm us down, before we went to eat. Then, after eating, we had to sit for at least ten minutes before going back to work. It worked. It also got me hooked on cigarettes, especially in any stressful situation. Of course, back in those days, they didn't know how harmful cigarette smoking was. Eventually, more SRNs came on board with experience, and students became proficient. But it was a few tough weeks for Margaret and I until that happened.

There was another catastrophe that happened during this time. We had a full operating schedule planned for the day, which was the normal fare. We now had a brand new instrument autoclave. This meant that we no longer had to lift the entire heavy instruments and pans, out of the boiling water sterilizers. This autoclave was positioned, so that once the door was opened, we could place the instruments on the trolleys, with the minimal amount of lifting, finish draping the trolleys, then they would be ready for each surgery as the day progressed. Because of the type of cases planned for this particular day, we had just about our entire stock of general instruments in the autoclave. The gauges read that it was ready to open the door. When I started to turn the wheel, it gave out this loud noise, and blew this thick cloud of white dust all across the waiting sterile trolleys. If that weren't bad enough, the door to the autoclave wouldn't open.

We had to cancel all the surgeries for the day. The clean up was massive. That white dust went everywhere. The company for the autoclave, sent someone down to fix it, and even they couldn't open the door! It was weeks before we got our instruments and the autoclave back. The hospital that was head of our district in Oxford sent us enough instruments to cover those that were locked away. We went back to using the boiling sterilizers, and were just thankful that we hadn't had them removed, until we saw how well the autoclave worked. Since that time I have never fully trusted any autoclave, and stand well to the side, whenever I have been the one to open the door.

The break-up with Pete was imminent about this time. I decided I wanted to travel and work in Africa, New Zealand and Australia. To do this, it was recommended to have more psychiatric nursing qualifications. Therefore I applied to, and was accepted by, Littlemore Hospital, for a year's post- graduate course in mental health, to start at the end of April 1962. Because I was an SRN, I would still be paid at the SRN rate. Not that the pay was that great even then. We got £44 a month before deductions, and we were paid monthly. My plan was to leave for Africa in the summer or 1963, with the thought of spending a couple of years each in all three countries.

Christmas was upon us, and being in the theatre, nothing was scheduled, so all we had to deal with was emergencies. This covered the whole week of Christmas and New Year. So we were free to visit the different wards, spend time with patients and colleagues, and decorate sister's office as if it was a cave, with stalagmites and stalactites, and the rhyme we made up about everyone.

We also spent time in the office, playing with an Ouija board. It seemed to work, but we weren't completely sold on it. While we were doing this one day, one of the surgical residents stopped by. He said the boards were too unreliable, and that in India palm reading was much better. He was from India, so we asked him if he could read palms. He said he could, so we all talked him into doing it for us. When he came to me, he said I would be meeting someone very soon, or had just met him, who had recently travelled across a large expanse of water. It would be a life time commitment, and that I needed to be careful. I asked him what I needed to be careful about. He would not enlarge on it. About fifteen months later I saw him in the hospital, and I had my baby daughter with me. He said; "See! I told you to be careful. You didn't listen." He asked me: "Where's your husband from?" I told him; America. Then I realized how accurate he was.

On 2nd January 1962, the weather was awful, with snow and icing everywhere. I was on call that night, when I received a phone call from one of my colleagues, Cookie. She was an American SRN. She had taken me to the New Years Eve dance at Upper Heyford, an American Airbase close by. I had never associated with any Americans before, and definitely never been to an Airbase. I had had a nice time, and the Americans there did not behave as badly as they did when they were in town; which was a big surprise!

The reason Cookie was calling, was that her friend's police squadron, was having their Christmas squadron party. and because of the weather, very few of the girls that had planned to go, could get through. Mainly because of the distances they were going to have to travel. She said; if I could round some girls up to come, they would pay the taxi fare, and get them back after the party. She knew I couldn't go because of being on call. I said I would do my best, but that they probably wouldn't be able to leave much before 8pm. She understood that.

The most I could get was three girls that didn't have prior commitments. Then another colleague, Ann Jones. who was from Australia, said that if Matron would allow it, she would take call for me, so I would make a fourth. Matron never allowed such a thing to happen, but I thought; nothing ventured, nothing gained. I asked and got permission. Then I had a mad scramble to get something acceptable to wear, and get ready by 8 pm. The trip in the taxi was interesting if not a little scary. It took us almost 2 hours to go 16 miles.

When we arrived, the four of us were greeted by, what seemed to be a room full of young men. Once tall one, with longer than usual black hair for an American, offered to take my coat. I passed it to him without thinking - he nearly dropped it from its unexpected weight! It was a full - length sheepskin coat, and somewhat heavier than the average coat; though I was quite used to it. He said afterwards, that he thought it was going to break his arm with the weight, and couldn't imagine how I could wear it.

It wasn't a large group; about thirty men, some with their wives or girlfriends. Cookies friends from the New Years Eve party were there, and her boyfriend, Alfonse Simpson, who hadn't been at the other party, because he had been working that night.

The tall fellow, with the dark hair, stayed right by my side. We talked, danced and had refreshments. I tried talking to others, but he persisted in staying right there. He seemed nice enough, but I just did not want to get stuck with just one person. It had only been a few weeks since Pete and I had broken up, and I just wanted to have some fun for a while. I had heard that, with Americans, if white girls danced with black men, the white men wouldn't have anything to do with her. So, when Simpson asked me to dance, I said yes. I figured it would probably put an end to this evening, but I wouldn't be stuck with just one person. When Simpson, (he preferred to be called Simpson), and I came off the dance floor, there was Mike waiting for me. Simpson says he isn't going to let you go. While Mike and I were dancing later, I thought; well at least he has nice eyes and after all it is only for one night.

The party was a lot of fun. One of the sergeants had a car, large enough to take us all back to the hospital, but he wanted someone to come with him, so that he had company coming back, in case he ran into trouble on the road. Mike volunteered. On the way back to the hospital, Mike asked me for a date for the following Saturday, to go to the movies. I am afraid I was mercenary enough, to only accept because I had no money left from Christmas expenses. So if I wanted to go out for the next few weeks, someone else was going to have to pay for it. He wanted to see the movie 'Guns of Navarone' that was playing in town. I told him I would meet him at a set time that I would be on time. If he wasn't there, I would look at the movie previews outside the theatre, then leave; that I did not wait for anyone. He said that was ok!

As I was walking across the zebra crossing, in front of the picture theatre on the following Saturday, someone quickly came across to meet me. He said "I am so glad you wore that coat. It made it easier for me to recognize you." I wondered what else he thought I would wear! He wasn't to know, that English nurses in those days, couldn't even dream of owning more than one coat at a time. The movie was very good, and we went for a drink at a local pub, before he walked me home. He said he was staying in town, so he wondered if we could see each other the next day.

He really seemed very nice. He wasn't loud, and he didn't brag as most GI's did at the time. In fact his name, Mike Griffis, sounded so British, and he dressed in a dark suit, and wore his hair as most Englishmen did at the time, instead of the crew cuts of the popular American style. I asked him if he really was from America. He assured me he was from Texas. I knew very little about American geography, so I asked him if that was up by New York. He informed me most emphatically that it was not! That Texans were rebels not Yankees. I told him; as far as we were concerned, if they were from America, they were Yanks. He learned to get used to that.

From that time on, we saw as much of each other as our work schedules would allow. After two weeks he asked me to marry him. I told him not to be such a fool. He wasn't much more than a baby. He said American men mature faster than English men do. I had no grounds or knowledge to agree or disagree.

Right about that time, I was sharing a flat with Pickers, and Margaret McCluskey. Pickers really preferred the convenience of living in the nurse's home, and was planning to move back in at the beginning of February. Margaret and I knew we could not afford the flat on our own. Mike said that, if we weren't able to find someone to move in, he would be willing to pay her share of the rent, if he could use the single room when he was in town. Over the next two weeks, Mike and I were together every time that was available to us. We just didn't like the time we were apart. He had been home and met the family. All seemed fine. Gran especially liked him - a big plus. His 21st birthday was coming up on February 1st. I made him a rush job birthday cake, and we planned a small party for him at the flat. He had continued to pester me to marry him. I agreed on his birthday. We called home to let the family know, and to ask Mum's permission, even though I was almost 22. It was safer that way! Mum blew her top! She said he was no longer welcome at her house, or in the village, and I wasn't to see him any more. I reminded her how old I was. She said it didn't make any difference. I was to do as I was told. I told her that wasn't going to happen. That in fact he was moving into the flat with Margaret and me, to help pay the rent.

We had a nice party for him, with our close friends, and didn't tell anyone what had transpired between Mum and us. We told Margaret later, and that Mum could cause problems. She said it was ok with her, and our landlady said the same thing. So Pickers moved out, and Mike moved in. Not a universally accepted practice in 1962; in fact not done at all. Mum had always said; "You never know a person until you live with them." Well I thought I could find out for myself, because I definitely did not want a marriage like my parents.

From this time on, my mother proceeded to do all in her power to break us up. She had made life difficult, for any other serious boyfriends I had ever had, but this time she went to new lengths. She started by writing, and then calling, the base commander, chaplain and adjutant; this to tell them to restrict Mike to base, and forbid him from seeing me. He was called to his squadron commanders' office concerning this, on several occasions. At first they asked the reason for her behaviour, how old I was, and how old he was. Then he told him our ages. They said we were both adults, and that nothing could be done. It was our choosing. The last time Mike was called in, the officer asked him if he really wanted to get tangled up with such a family. Mike told him he was marrying me, not my mother!

Finally, towards the end of March, Mum changed her mind, and said if I insisted, and if I wanted to get married in Aynhoe church, she wouldn't stop me. We went to see the vicar to arrange for banns etc. That afternoon we went to the pictures. When we returned home, Mum had changed her mind again and was not going to allow it.

At the end of March, Gene Bush, a friend of Mike's, wanted to go to London for the weekend to see the sites. We arranged to stay at the Strand Palace. At that time, a room there only cost £7. We got to show Gene a lot of London, but he wanted to see more. This meant staying another night. The only place that had a room available, was a guest house down by Paddington Station. There was one bed available in a room with 2 other men, and a room with 5 single beds and a crib in it. Gene took the one with the men, and Mike and I took the other room. I checked all the beds, to see if it looked like they had changed the sheets, since the last time they were used. Only one bed had clean sheets. Luckily, Mike and I were pretty skinny at that time, so we shared the same bed. That was 31st March, going into April Fools Day. Now I know what is meant by April Fools! If you get pregnant at that time, you spend the next Christmas in the hospital - having a baby!

Mike with nice eyes

I started at Littlemore Hospital shortly after this, to do my mental nurse training. I was there less than a month. It was definitely not the type of nursing I was interested in. The smells there were nauseating. I have always been very sensitive to smells, and not being able to communicate in any type of constructive way, was more than difficult for me to deal with. I admire anyone that can. I recognized very quickly that it wasn't for me, so I resigned. They only required one weeks notice.

At the beginning of May, I returned home to Aynhoe on Mum's invitation, with plans to look for other work. By this time, Mike and I had started the paperwork process, that was required for us to get married. We were aiming for 12th June, and then it had to be delayed until 23rd, because the paperwork was taking longer than expected. It was finally 7th July. In the meantime, we realised I was pregnant.

While I am home looking for work, Mum started to really give me a difficult time about Mike. She wouldn't let him near the house. During this time I would call Mike, just to talk to someone sane. I would meet him away from the village with my scooter, and we would go for picnics in the rain, or go to the USO club and play games, just to be in the dry and warm. Neither of us had any money, so we had to find something that didn't cost anything.

He wanted to come over and get me out of the house, but I knew that wasn't possible. During this time Dad was friendly with Mum, so he would never do anything to jeopardize his standing with her, and Gran was helpless to help me. June and Norman were working, and rarely at home. At the beginning of June, I finally found a temporary job at one of the private girls' boarding schools in the area, as an assistant matron. It was a live-in position. I had private quarters, so Mike was able to visit. It was warm, dry and safe. They knew we planned to get married as soon as the paperwork came through. I must admit it was a relief to be there. Our paperwork finally came through, with the final signature on the paper, on 6th July, so we could go ahead with our plans, to get married on the 7th.

The family, including my parents, knew when the wedding was to be, and where. Mum had forbidden any member of the family to attend. Hilary and a co worker, Angela Burgess, agreed to be our witnesses. Mike had rented a small 8 foot by 28 foot caravan for us to move into, in a trailer park just off the base, so we wouldn't need a car. He had arranged for 2 taxis, to go to the Registrars Office in Bodicote, to bring us all back. I had gone to Banbury to have my hair done. On the way to the bus stop, I saw Mum and Dad, and begged them to come to my wedding. She refused, and said she didn't need to bother, because it wouldn't last 6 months. Dad said nothing. I missed my bus and had to get a taxi back to the school. When I got there, imagine my surprise. June was there. She said she had to sneak out in her work clothes, so Mum wouldn't suspect, and she thought others were coming. By this time Hilary and Angela were there, and we were running late. I had made a simple blue dress for the occasion. They all helped me get dressed, and get my makeup on. One of the taxis came to pick us up. The taxi drivers were an elderly couple from Croughton. They were dressed for a wedding, and they brought enough corsages for several people. I had my own of 3 salmon roses. When we got to the Registrars Office, Mike was there with Suzanne, and Norman walked up right after. They had all come in their work clothes, so Mum would not suspect. After we were married, as we came out of the building, Jill, Suzanne's sister, arrived. Jill and Suzanne are Kath's daughters from her first marriage. Afterwards, when the pictures were taken of everyone, we included the taxi drivers, Mr and Mrs Moore, because they said we needed mature people there. They knew Mum, and what she had done to us, and were trying to make it up to us. We thought it was very kind of them, plus they wouldn't take any money for the taxis. We all went back to the trailer, where we had a few refreshments for everyone, and I had made a small wedding cake.

Our home was made up of 3 rooms. The living/dining room, in this was a built in sofa that could be made into a bed. A built in cabinet between the door and the sofa, a coal/wood stove, a table and 2 chairs. There was a sun vent in the roof. The door led into the kitchen, which was really just a passageway to the bedroom. The kitchen had a sink that was 10" x 8" and 6" deep. The stove had 2 burners on top, and an oven without a thermostat. Opposite the stove, was a door to a storage cupboard. The bedroom had another built in sofa that we left permanently down as a bed. There were two built-in cabinets on either side of the door, and a narrow cabinet above the window over the bed.

Whenever it rained, this narrow cabinet would fill up with water, and then dump it onto the bed. So we slept with a raincoat on the bed, so we could gather it up and dump it out of the door. There was a shed outside. Half was for storage, the other half was an outside toilet - it did flush!

The next day, I planned to cook; roast chicken, stuffing, potatoes, vegetables and gravy, and for desert, gooseberry pie and custard. All was going well, by using the table in the living/dining room to do the preparations. I had just lined the pie plate with the pastry, and put the gooseberries in it, when the sun beating down on the back of my neck through the sun vent, became too much for me and I fainted. The only problem was, my feet and legs were in the living room, my trunk was in the kitchen, and my head and shoulders were in the bedroom. Mike couldn't figure out how to get to my head without hurting me. After I came to, I finished the pie and then rested. Mike pretty much finished the rest of the meal. Surprisingly the dinner was good. I gave Mike a large piece of the pie with plenty of custard on it. He took a large spoonful, and said: "Oh! This is good." I took a bite and nearly choked on it! I had forgotten to put any sugar in it. To this day, I have no idea how Mike kept a straight face when he tasted it.

Because of our limited funds, we didn't even have a radio, so Mike would check books out of the library and read to me while I knitted baby clothes. One day, he said he wanted to learn how to knit - he made a cardigan for the baby. He did a good job of it. Eventually we were able to buy a radio. This was how we could both knit at the same time.

I taught him how to play gin rummy; he was so determined to beat me, sometimes we would be playing into the small hours of the morning. We were saving for a cot for the baby; we had no idea how to buy a pram. We had thought about selling my scooter. I only had 5 more payments on it, so it was a possibility. I couldn't ride it any more, because of some of the complications I was having during the pregnancy, so it was just sitting there.

Dad turned up one day and wanted to talk to Mike. They went off in Dad's car down the road. About 45 minutes later he dropped Mike off. Mike said Mum had sent him out to talk to him, to tell Mike she wanted him to apologise to Mum for marrying me, then she would forgive us. He told him to go back to her, tell her not to send her errand boy to do her dirty work, and that neither of us have anything to apologise for. If she wants to see us, she will have to accept that. A couple of weeks later, she turned up on our doorstep, with a basket of vegetables from their garden, and acted as if nothing had happened. This was a common practice of how she dealt with things, never an apology or explanation.

Chapter 8

The Between Years

The living conditions in the trailer got worse, as the weather became colder, along with the complications in my pregnancy, including losing weight because of vomiting so much. Unbeknownst to us, Mum talked to Denis, to see if we could move in with him until after the baby was born. Gran was living up at Mum's, because it was easier to care for her there. Denis agreed it would be better for all, if we did move in with him, and he would like the company. The only way we could, was if Mike could get a ride to work; he was able to do that without too much difficulty. In October we moved into 20 Aynhoe.

Before this happened, we confirmed with Denis that he really wanted us to, knowing his feelings towards Americans. He said he did, and would enjoy having others living in the house. We tried to be as unobtrusive as possible, and yet to make it cosy and homelike again. I found out he liked to eat porridge for breakfast, so I made it the old fashioned way. I would put it on the stove the night before, in a double boiler, and let it simmer all night. This way it was thick and creamy for all of us, when we got up in the morning. Denis really appreciated it. He also said it was nice, coming home from work to a warm house that felt lived in again. It hadn't been that way since Gran had moved into Mum's. By this time Kath had been divorced for some time, and her and Den were dating pretty seriously; so most of his evenings were spent with her. Living in a more stable situation, my health improved, but the vomiting didn't.

Denis wouldn't take any rent from us, so we worked on trying to buy a car. In November, I only had one more payment on my scooter Mum said she would like to buy it from us for Norman. She would make the last payment and give me the money to buy a pram. We agreed. Mike and I went to Banbury to look at prams. The ones that we liked were about £ 40- 50. I liked the ones with the large wheels at the back, especially the burgundy colour. We went home and told Mum. She said we didn't need to bother looking. She had already bought one for us from Mrs. Thurgood for £20. She said to give her £19 and to use the other £1 for a dress for the baby. I told Mum that wasn't the agreement; she had said a pram, not a second hand one. The scooter was worth over £100, and that wasn't fair. Mum would not budge. The papers had all been signed over, so I didn't have any recourse.

She had stuck me again. The pram was ok. It was navy blue, and the back wheels were only slightly larger than the front. But it was used and not what we wanted. Then, to add insult to injury, when Mrs. Thurgood was at Mum's getting her hair done, Mum said; show her one of the dresses you have got for the baby, and tell her it was the one you got with the pound she gave you. I refused! I said; not until I have the pound in my pocket. Mum called me an ungrateful. I never saw the pound.

We were able to buy a car from the local VW dealer. The only way we were able to get a loan through the base, was if it was a new one. So we got a left hand drive, with the thought that we could have it shipped back to the States when we left. The government would pay for the shipping. We picked it up from the dealer on 19th December. The dealer scratched the back fender backing it out of the garage. He told us to bring it back after Christmas and they would repair it. It was a grey VW beetle. 21st December, we went to the Base for groceries, and to pick up Gene Bush, with plans for him to spend the day with us. Coming back on the outskirts of Souldern, we were going to stop for petrol, because they were selling it for 3d a gallon cheaper than anywhere else. We were waiting to turn right into the station, when a car crested the top of the hill in the middle of the road in front of us. We didn't stand a chance. He hit us head on, turned us, and carried us about 50 yards down the road, before we broke loose. He continued going and took out about 20 feet of hedge. When it happened, all I could think about was to keep the car away from my abdomen, so I pushed onto the dashboard with all my strength. They said afterwards I did it with so much strength, that I bent the frame outwards, causing the windscreen to pop out, and bend inwards breaking down the middle. It hit my face, broke my nose and lacerated my face. I later found I had cracked my ribs, sprained my knee and wrist, and for weeks had the impression of my stockings on my legs. Mike was unhurt and Gene was shook up. The car was a mess. The police and witnesses said it was obviously not our fault. The people at the station said the car could be left there until after Christmas. The important thing was, to get me to the Base hospital to be checked out. Before we left, the police told us, when the case went to court we would be fine, as long as it didn't end up in Bicester court. If it did, we wouldn't stand a chance. The reason being, that the magistrate there got pregnant by an American, who left her with it, and no American left that court innocent. It could have gone to any of three courts, because of where it happened. You will see the result later in this Chapter. We spent 4-5 hours at the base hospital, mainly because they could not hear the baby's heartbeat. There wasn't much they could do for me, except clean me up. Finally the situation was stable, and the Air police got us, and our groceries, a ride home. Mike was in the Air Police.

When we got back home, Mum and Kath were busy with the hairdressing. Some friends of ours, Pat and Joe Delaney, were visiting with Gran in the living room. I stayed in the kitchen, Mike went in and explained to Gran what had happened, and that the baby and I were fine. Pat and Joe came out to check on me, and Dad and Den came home about that time. We decided the best thing I could do, was to go into the saloon, so Mum and Kath could see I was OK, but a bit of a mess. I walked in and stood beside Mum. She turned and looked at me and said "You silly bugger what have you got on?" She thought I had a mask on, then she realised it was my face. I told her "Its OK. You see I'm OK." After everyone was convinced we were alright, we went down home to rest.

At 1 am that night, I started with labour pains. An hour later they were a minute long and 2 minutes apart. We went up home and woke Mum and Dad, so Dad could take us to the hospital in Bicester, where we were scheduled to have the delivery. I was determined to have a natural delivery, even with my injuries. The midwife and doctor said they would have to see how things went. The other patients thought Mike had beaten me up, because by now, the bruising was extensive all over my face. The nurses set them right. The labour was very erratic, but the last 24 hours of the, by then, 62 hours since it had started, were classified as hard labour. I was extremely tired, and felt that if I could just sleep for a while, I'd be OK. The doctor examined me, and said I had to go urgently by ambulance, to the Radcliffe in Oxford. That my cervix had not dilated, that my uterus had gone into inertia, and the next thing that will happen, was that my uterus would go tonic. It would kill the baby, and then I would haemorrhage and die. Mike came in the ambulance with me. When we arrived at the hospital, we were met by 3 physicians. They examined me going down the hall, in the lift, and into the theatre. I saw them look at each other and saw that the surgeon had meconium from the baby in his hand. I asked them if I could get some rest, then still have a normal delivery. He said: "You will be dead in 20 minutes if we don't operate, and the baby is at great risk." We went into the anaesthetic room. Mr. Stallworthy, the head of the department, was on call for emergencies and he was called out from a formal dinner, therefore he came wearing a formal dinner suit, and he told me he would be operating. I told the anaesthetist to be careful of my nose, because of the pain associated with the accident. She started to give me the pentathol, and then I remembered to tell her that it didn't work on me. Stallworthy told her to give me more. It still didn't work. It really threw her. She said she would have to put me under with the gas. She forgot my nose. I grabbed her hand and said watch it. The next thing I knew, I was still in the anaesthetic room, but much smaller. Mike was with me, and I told the nurse I was so thirsty. She got me a jug of water, and before she came back with a glass, I had drunk it all straight from the jug. She went and got me another one. I felt fine. They said we had a little girl. She was 20" long, weighed 5 lb 10 ozs, and that she had very long hair, but no nails, or hair on her eyebrows or eyelashes. This is typical of a premature birth. I told them; this is 24th December, and that is when she is due. Later they said, considering the date you got married, why do you insist she is a term baby instead of taking the premature label? I said because this is when she was due.

That evening I felt so good. I was up on my knees getting things from the foot of the bed. The nurses said: "How can you do that when you just had surgery?" I said; because I feel great. Mike left to go home, to let them know all was ok, and to telegram his parents. The next day Mr. Stallworthy came by. He told me that my c-section was the fastest he had ever done. It was 10 minutes from skin to skin, and it wouldn't have taken that long, but my uterus was wrapped around the baby's neck, and it took some time to get it loose without damaging my uterus. He said, when he closed, all looked good, the baby was doing fine, and would be up to me soon. They just want to monitor her breathing a bit longer.

They had put me in a private room, because of my situation and because of my car injuries. They brought the baby to me just after lunch. Her hair was about 3 inches long, and stood straight out from her head. She was so long and skinny, she looked like a ferret with big eyes. I said so to the nurse. She thought I was terrible to say such a thing. I said; well it is true. I had said from the beginning, that she was going to be called Jane Leslie. I looked at her and thought; no, that doesn't fit her. She is a Jane Terrie, and so she was. Later that day Mike, and the whole family except Gran, came to visit me, and they let the baby stay in the room, as long as they didn't pick her up, and they wore masks.

When I looked out of my bedroom window the next morning, there was about 4 feet of snow on the ground, and everything in England had ground to a halt. I got a message from Mike, that he couldn't make it up that day, but would try the next day. He arrived just after lunch the next day. He had walked the 23 miles from Aynhoe to Oxford. We couldn't afford for him to stay over, so he walked back again that night. He did that every day until New Years Eve. By then I had told one of the doctors what he was doing, and he wouldn't stop.

During Mike's visits, Jane stayed in the room with us. Mike has always had a way with babies, and has a real knack with them; so he usually held her for a while during his visits. One day, when he was holding her, the Sister came into the room. When she saw Mike holding the baby, she said," What is he doing holding that baby? He has no right to do that." I snapped back at her, "He has more right to hold her than anyone else here does." She looked daggers at me, and left the room.

The trouble with the weather was, that it just kept on snowing for weeks. I was so worried about Mike walking that distance everyday, that I wanted them to discharge me. We were told the train service was being opened to Banbury the next day, and that most of the roads had one lane open. They said if he arranged for a taxi to take me to the train station, and one at the other end to get me to Banbury, then we could go. Jane was 6 lbs by now, so they weren't concerned about her. All was set, and Mike was able to find a place to stay that we could afford for the night. When we got to the train station, the train was running an hour and half late. The heat had failed in the carriage we got in, and it was freezing. They stopped the train along the tracks, so we could move to one of the other carriages. Without a platform, the step down and up is extremely steep; even without a baby bundled up in your arms, and me having just had abdominal surgery. By the time we got to Banbury, we were over two hours late, and the taxi had long given up. We had another long wait for another one. Finally we got home, and Gran was, for the first time, able to see and hold her first Great Grand daughter, she was so proud.

Jane was a good baby during the day, with long walks in her pram and being outside the front door in her pram, she slept most of the time. When nighttime came she was a different baby. She screamed almost all night, no matter what we did. We were concerned about Denis but he never complained. Three weeks into this, where nothing would pacify her, we were exhausted. This one night, Mike, in desperation, paddled her butt twice through blankets, sleeping suit and her napkin. She obviously did not feel anything more than the sudden jolt from it. She took a couple of deep breaths and stopped screaming. She stopped crying, never to do it again at night.

Because of the weather, we had to dry all her clothes, nappies, sheets and our clothes in front of the open fire. This was before disposable napkins. The moisture in the room was like a sauna. We had an electric copper for boiling the white clothes, and a cold water tap that ran into the washhouse, and a small emersion heater over the sink in the pantry, for limited hot water. The toilet was still up the long walk, and there was still no bathroom in the house. Within a week, Mike and I had streaming colds, and trying not to infect the baby was not easy. After a month Mike had to go back to work. Oh! You remember the car? Well it was, of course, still at the service station where we had had the accident, under many feet of snow. They weren't able to get to it until April. Then it was taken to a non VW dealer to be repaired who welded all the parts together. Apparently with VW they just latch or lock together. They aren't welded. The only time the car did not squeak so loud that people would turn to look at it, was when it was raining, and Mike could drive it through large puddles. Of course, with our luck, we went to Bicester court, found guilty of negligence and fined £174. That was a lot of money. In those days it was over a months pay.

The doctors had said, it would be better if we waited as long as possible to have another baby, considering my complications during pregnancy, and with the birth, that my uterus needed time to heal. The birth control pills had become available, under very close monitoring and for cases like mine. They could only be obtained through certain clinics. My doctor gave me a referral, only it was to the wrong clinic. By the time I got to the right clinic, and was given the pills, I was pregnant again.

Because the British medical system had born the cost of my first pregnancy, I thought it only fair for the Americans to have the cost this time. I went to the clinic on Base. They sent for my records from the Radcliffe, and immediately made me an appointment at the main Base Hospital at Burdrop Park in Wiltshire. The outcome for that was, that I was going to have to go there every week until I was delivered. That I was not to ride the bus put on by the base, because it took all day. Mike was to be excused from work every week to take me down there. The base did not like this at all.

The good side of all of this was, that with the weekly blood and urine tests, they were able to treat the kidney infections, and other problems before they got as bad as before. They found that, if they changed my nausea pills each week, I didn't vomit, so I was able to gain some weight. The baby was due on 23rd February, but they wanted to do the c-section on the 13th so there was no risk of me going into labour. I asked if it could be the 12th or 14th so she could have her own birthday, because mine was the 13th. They elected to do it the 14th.

Jane Terrie 11 months

Jane in the meantime, was growing well. She never lost her hair as most babies do. It turned blonde, and was down to her shoulders and very thick. By the time she was 11 months old, she was already potty trained and walking. She liked sweet things. Because of this additional pregnancy, we knew we needed to move, and Denis wanted to start the renovation of the house, for him and Kath for when they got married. We found a large ground floor apartment in Deddington, and moved in in August. We borrowed a truck from the base, and moved ourselves in the pouring rain. It was a beautiful summer, and there was a lovely garden in the back of the house. The only problem was, there was only one bedroom.

There was another couple there that were from London, and they had been looking for another place to live. They asked us if we found a house large enough for 2 families, would we be willing to share with them. We said; only if it was large enough not to be on top of each other and we had our own bathrooms. We started to look and found a house that fitted what we needed. It was £30 pounds a month but between us it would be only £15 a month. Considerably less than we were paying. The 2nd floor had 2 very large bedrooms and a bathroom. The 1st floor had a very large bedroom, and above the huge living room was a room used for storage, but could have been changed into another living room and a full bathroom. The ground floor had a very large living room, entrance hall, and a very large country kitchen, with a large table and chairs in the middle. The back was just a concrete courtyard, looking over a farmyard. The front and one side had a fenced garden. It was in the village of Charlton, with a post office, shop, pub, church, and a school. We all agreed it was worth it. We signed for it and moved in. Everything was going well, and we all thought we'd be able to save money living there. A month later we came downstairs, to find the other couple had moved out, left us a set of dishes in payment for what they owed us, (it didn't cover it) and a note saying they missed London too much, and were returning there. There wasn't any way we could afford the house on our own. Mike advertised on-base for another couple to share with us. A GI from Indiana was expecting his wife to join him in a few days, so they took it. Their names were Dixie and Dick. They were what I would call thick! It was almost impossible to hold any kind of a conversation with her. Dick was only marginally better. I tried to show her how things worked, especially the copper vs the washing machine. She ended up with white clothes, all colours of the rainbow, and stretched out of all reason. I remember one day trying to talk about butterflies. She proceeded to tell me that Moths grew into butterflies. There was no convincing her otherwise.

After 4 months they found themselves a house on their own. By this time we had just over a month left on the lease. We told them we were shipping out, was the reason for leaving before the contract.

We found a newly built 3 bedroom bungalow in Tackley, so that we could move in just before Christmas. It was cheaper than anything else we could find. At first the plumbing was not completed in the bathroom, but at least we had a chemical toilet to tide us over. All the rooms were light, and a good size. The kitchen only had cabinets in the sink unit, but there was plenty of room for cabinets to be put in it. We found a kitchen type Welsh Dresser that worked very well, along with a drop leaf table that we could use as a work top, and dining chairs. We rented a refrigerator, which was larger than the average at the time, so that made up for no larder. The living room was large, as was the entrance hall. The hall turned out to be a good place for the children to play, when the weather was bad. There were 2 double bedrooms, and a larger than usual single bedroom. There were extensive gardens in the front, back, and side, but it looked like a construction site. The owner said he would level plough and put it right for us. But he never quite found the time for it! So even with our limited efforts, the garden was always something I was ashamed of.

We had excellent neighbours all around us, and the people in the village were all friendly and kind. The closest ones were the ones that lived next door, Zena and Pete Smith, and their two girls Elizabeth and Rebecca. Zena was Polish, and had been interred in a concentration camp early on in the war, when she was only 13, until they were liberated in 1945. She was 17 then, and Pete was one of the ones that liberated her. She always had problems with digestion. She felt it was the time of starvation in the camp that caused it. She was never able to locate her family after the war. She was one of the thousands of non-Jews that suffered the same fate they did. She said they used to lie in their bunks at night, and pray for the bombs to drop on them, to put them out of their misery.

Penny Lynn was born 14th February 1964 6 lbs 10 ozs. Her name was totally Mike's choice. I had been told I could not have any more children, because of pregnancy complications. I was so angry she wasn't a boy, that I would have nothing to do with her. Mike, and the nurses, would tell me how cute she was, but to no avail. Then one day the nurse came to my room, dumped the baby on my bed, and said we are too busy. You are going to have to feed her today. I held her head in my left hand in front of me, and fed her with my right hand. In this position I could see her face well. My thought was; well at least she looks like Mike. She took her bottle well without fussing. A far cry from Jane's eating habit at that age. Then she burped so easily, not taking half an hour to do it like Jane did. After she had finished drinking, I let her lay on my lap on the bed. She slept for quite a while, and then she started fussing a bit, so I put her on my chest to pat her back. Jane used to hate being that close to anyone. Even when she was first born, she would get her arms between you and her, and push you away. Penny instead just snuggled down to get more comfortable, and then snuggled her head into my neck and went to sleep. I felt like an absolute heel for being the way I was towards her! Penny has remained the same all her life: Affectionate, caring and always up for a cuddle. So we had two girls. So what! Maybe we will have grandsons!

Jane took to Penny immediately and seemed fascinated by her. So fascinated, she went back to needing nappies and refused to walk. One day the District Nurse asked me if Jane had reverted back to the pre-Penny life style. I told her; "No I don't think she will until Penny does." Jane was in ear shot of this conversation. When we got home, I carried Jane into the living room and left her on the floor. After getting Penny out of the pram, I turned around, and there was Jane standing behind me, just to prove me wrong. This turned out to be typical Jane; she does things when she is ready to, not before.

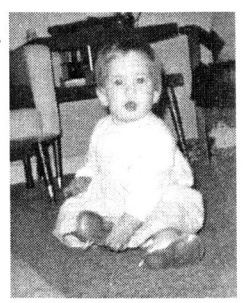

*Penny Lynn
8 months*

Tackley turned out to be a very nice friendly village. Our neighbours were all that you could ask: Friendly, caring, helpful and not intrusive. The local shops had all we needed on a daily basis, and the delivery people were much the same as we had had in Aynhoe. Oxford was closer, and at that time parking in Oxford was easy, and usually cost nothing. There was an American type Laundromat in Summertown, on our side of Oxford, that was ideal for our needs. It was clean, and the owners were always there and so helpful and friendly.

Tackley had 2 pubs. One was very old, and the inside looked like it hadn't changed much from the medieval times; with flag stone floors and the bare minimum in furnishings. The other was more the village pub, with dartboard and bar billiards in the bar section, and patrons playing dominos or draughts. The lounge was small, warm and cosy, with overstuffed comfortable furniture. The landlord and landlady were friendly and well liked. There was a nice garden to sit in, in the summer, if you wanted to bring your whole family. In those days, children under 17 were not allowed inside the pubs.

One of the local farmers had his fields on the outskirts of the village, just past our house. He had the delightful name of Abel Honor. Of course, the 'H' was dropped when you said his name. He always had time to stop his tractor for a friendly word when he saw you. Mike and he developed quite a friendship. So much so, that when Abel was haymaking, Mike offered to help, even though Mike suffered badly with hay fever. Within two days of working in the fields, Mike's face was so swollen he could barely open his eyes. It was so bad the base put him on quarters, (off sick). Mike was able to go back to helping Abel before he was able to go back to work! I told him: "This is probably either going to kill or cure you of hay fever." It cured him! He has only been minimally bothered by it ever since. Abel paid him well - in eggs - for all his work. Mike enjoyed it so much. I think it was the feeling of belonging to a community as much as anything.

The situation with the family in Aynhoe continued with its ups and downs. June was living and working in Oxford. She, and most of her friends, were usually full of energy, but no money to do too much. Quite often, she and a group of her friends, would catch the last train to Tackley; descend on us for a warm house, free food and drinks, then a free ride back to Oxford, usually after 1 am. They usually brought someone with a guitar for entertainment. June at the time was engaged to Tony Morris. He had attended Headington School at the same time as us, and then had gone on to graduate from the Royal Academy of Art in London. He was already quite an accomplished artist, but still very poor.

The only other big change that took place during this time was that Mike left the Air Police and cross trained into Supply. After Penny was born, it became harder for me to stay up and wait for Mike to come home after working until midnight, so that we could spend time, sharing our day's activities with each other. Then I had a real bad cold, and found staying awake even harder. I must have just fallen asleep when he came home. He had had a bad day, and was really upset to find me asleep. We had our first of the two big arguments we have had in our marriage. In the morning he got up and left the house in his uniform. This was strange, because he never wore it when he was off duty. He didn't return until well after lunch. He then told me what he had done. He went to see his squadron commander, and told him he had had his first fight with his wife, all because of the crap he had to put

Penny 11 months, Jane 2 years

up with at work. So he had come to tell them: "I quit." There had been several Air Policemen that had had breakdowns over the past few weeks. So his commander thought was another case of that. They got him to the dispensary, to see the psychiatrist, and the doctor realised he wasn't the same as the others. The outcome was, he recommended Mike be cross-trained, into a less stressful job. Now he would work 8 to 5, Monday to Friday. To actually have a normal scheduled life, even for a short time, was a real treat. It gave us the chance to let Mike see more of England, and to attempt to satisfy his insatiable interest in English history.

Chapter 9

Goodbye to England

Mike was part of the base that was called SAC, or Strategic Air Command. It is a known fact, that once you are in SAC, you never get out of it. Sometime before Christmas 1964, we knew all SAC bases in England were being closed down. It was like a huge Exodus. The police and supply were 2 of the last groups to leave. We were all being shipped back like cattle.

I had to get a visa, which meant an overnight trip to the American Embassy, and Mike had to go with me because he was my sponsor. June and Tony offered to take care of the girls. By this time Jane was 2 and Penny a year old. Let me say this much; at this point in time, it was just as well Tony was there, with some understanding of what infants need!

We were scheduled to leave England on 13th April 1965. When Mum heard this, she said she would like to have us stay with them, for the month before we left. That way the family would get to spend as much time as possible with us and the girls. This meant arranging for our household goods to be picked up, a month ahead of time. All was arranged without too much difficulty, and we gave notice to our landlord.

Mum was going to come over the night before the movers arrived, to take all our stuff that was to travel with us, over to her house. In addition, all our extra food and cleaning stuff would go with her at the same time. We would have enough for that night and in the morning for the girls, and whatever cleaning stuff we needed to clean the house, after the movers had gone. Mum was to come first thing in the morning to pick the girls up. After the movers had gone and we had cleaned the house our neighbours would take us over to Mum's. Mike had arranged a ride from Aynhoe to work each day, with someone that worked his hours, and passed through Aynhoe each day. We had sold the car because it never quite worked right after the accident.

All went as planned, and Mum was quite excited when she picked everything up the night before, and talked about how nice it was going to be for everyone.

By 8 am the next morning there was still no sign of Mum. The movers had arrived, so I went down to the phone box to call Mum, and find out what was happening. Mum answered the phone and I asked if there was something wrong with the car. She said 'No!' So I asked when she was coming to pick up the girls. She said she wasn't. I asked her what she meant. She said she had changed her mind she didn't want us over there. I said: "But Mum you have all our food, all ours and the girls' things, and the movers are here, and we are supposed to be out of the house tonight." She told me that was my problem not hers. I also reminded her we no longer had a car to pick up our belongings. She told me I'd have to work it out. She hung up!

After I told Mike what had happened, he said he'd call the base, and see if they would have a place on base we could stay, or if they'd put us up in a hotel. Our next door neighbour, Zena, said she would take care of the girls for the day. Mike had no luck on the base. They couldn't put us up in a hotel, until we had only ten days left before leaving the country. Our landlord said we could stay there until that time, if we could find enough stuff to survive in the house. All our neighbours rallied to help they came up with 3 camp beds, and a cot for Penny, and all the linen needed. They loaned us a table, chairs, and a couple of arm chairs, and enough pots pans and dishes for us to get by. The house echoed a bit. But there were lots of open spaces for the girls to play with toys that were lent to us. That evening the fish and chip van came round, so we had supper, and I had been able to get cereal and milk from the shop for breakfast. Of course, during all this, we are still having to deal with the movers. But as soon as they realised what had happened to us, they were the best, kindest and most helpful movers we have ever had.

Of course, we still had to get all of our belongings from over at Mums. I called her, and said Pete our neighbour would bring us over. She wanted to know when it would be. I told her, and she said that it would all be waiting at the top of the steps for me in the front garden. I asked her why all this, and why had she changed her mind. She said: "If you don't know, I'm not telling you". I didn't know why, and she didn't tell me until 25 years later. Then she told me that she thought if she was to do this, I would leave Mike and wouldn't leave England. By the time she told me this, she knew she was wrong, and that she shouldn't have done it.

Ten days before we were due to leave England, the base moved us into a hotel in Bicester. We had said goodbye to our very special friends and neighbours in Tackley. Tony Morris came to visit us – to say goodbye, and give us a watercolour he had done for us of the Radcliffe Camera in Oxford. June and Tony had parted company by this time.

I called home several times, to try to get Mum to at least see us, so we could say goodbye to everyone. She would not change her mind. I said to her; you can't let me leave without even saying goodbye to Gran. She said that is up to you. I managed to reach Kath and Den, and they told me when Mum and Dad would be gone, so I could get into the house to see Gran. It was just a few days before we were leaving. Mike borrowed a car, and we all drove over there. We were able to spend a couple of hours with Gran. She didn't know we were coming, but she was so happy to see us; she said she was so frightened she wasn't going to ever see us again. She said she had no idea what had got into Mum, and that she didn't think she would ever understand her. One of the hardest things I had to do in my life, was to say goodbye and leave Gran that day, knowing full well I would never see her again.

I knew that Mum and Dad were aware of the time we would be leaving on the bus from Upper Heyford. I did not believe they would actually let us leave the country without saying goodbye. They did. Then I was unrealistic, and thought that maybe they found out when we were leaving Mildenhall, and they would be there. They weren't.

When I agreed to marry Mike, I did it only when I felt that he was important enough to me, that I could leave England, knowing full well I would never be able to return. I have always loved England and have always been very proud to be English. In reality, I am English through and through. For better or for worse I will take England, and I have always felt that way. Therefore that day was a very traumatic one for me. Plus, other than Mike, I was leaving the one person who had stood by me, and loved me unconditionally for who I was, Gran.

As we arrived at Mildenhall, I noticed a plane over on the runway that looked a little the worse for wear. I pointed it out to Mike. He said it was probably the one the fire crews use, to practice putting fires out. That looked about right to me.

After we, 'the cattle', were all processed, we were loaded onto another bus to take us to the plane. It was the one Mike thought was used for fire drills! It was a cargo plane, a turbo prop, which had been used in the Berlin airlift. When fitted with seats it was supposed to have 99 people in it. They had squeezed in 129, and military people have no baggage limits!

We were one of the last from our bus to walk towards the plane. I did not hurry and I did not take my eyes off of the tarmac. It was as if I was willing it to stay attached to my feet. When I got to the point that I had to climb the steps, I looked at the ground and thought; "Good bye my England, goodbye, I do love you so much and I will always miss you." I climbed the steps with the tears silently streaming down my face. That was the hardest thing I have ever done in my life.

Chapter 10

The Horton - 44 Years Later

In 1988 I had the opportunity go by the Horton to see it, and to see if anyone was there that I knew. When I walked into the entrance, it was like a deserted ghost town in Colorado. Where the hub of the hospital had been – the telephone operator's desk was a gift shop. There were very few people walking around, instead of the usual bustle in a hospital, it echoed, it needed painting, it was shabby.

Someone asked me who I was looking for- I explained why I was there. They said Sister Stewart and Holbech Ward were still there, to go down and see her. Holbech and Sister Stewart were as I remembered them, and she remembered me. She said there were great changes going on. The SEN student nurses were not of the calibre they were when it was SRN training. Later she called someone in the front nursing office to see me. That person remembered me, but I really didn't remember her. She said that there were no longer Matrons, instead now they were called Nursing Officers. I asked why – she had no idea. The only good thing about the visit really was I joined the Hortonian, a club for previous Horton workers. I regretted going back.

Now I think it is good that I made the visit, because I can now compare it with the Horton of today, 44 years after I left the confines and security of my training hospital.

The Horton General Hospital, or as it is known today 'The Horton Hospital', is still the vital hub of the community, as the local hospital of not just northern Oxfordshire; but of the villages, and towns in the surrounding counties, of Northamptonshire and Warwickshire. The area is fondly known by the locals as Banburyshire; officially there is no such place, except in the hearts of the people who have lived there for many a long year.

When the hospital was recently threatened with closure, there was considerable rallying towards the hospital. This has always happened when it has been threatened by outsiders, since long before my time. I did e-mail from the States, stating that I supported the Horton remaining open, because it has always been vital to the large local community it serves.

I have listened to the local people voice their fears of losing their local hospital, as is common throughout the entire country. According to everyone I talked to, the Horton is still the hospital that gives the best care with the most caring staff. It is clean, and everyone is proud of it, and they fully support it. What is still being said, is that the Nurses and Doctors are great. That sure sounded like the Horton I knew, and was so proud to have trained at. Then Hilary, my life long friend told me about a friend of hers in Oxford, who recently needed surgery. The staff at the John Radcliffe told her, that it would be over a year before they would be able to do it. But if she was willing to go to the Horton in Banbury, she could have it done much sooner. She chose this, knowing nothing about the Horton. After her stay at the Horton, she said she was so impressed with the care she received, and that she was treated as a person not a number. In future she intended to use the Horton, whenever she can. The other thing that impressed her, was how clean it was, just like the hospitals were years ago.

On hearing all of these accolades, I had to see the Horton again, and put an unplanned chapter at the end of this book. I contacted the Hospital Director, Mike Fleming, to explain about the book, and what I wanted to do. He very graciously invited me to see the entire hospital, and meet anyone I wanted to, for this final chapter.

On my first trip, I was able to visit all of the old parts of the hospital, with Yolanda Jacob, Mike Fleming's Executive Assistant as my guide. No longer was the old entrance drab, or shabby. The walls were painted pale blue with royal blue doors and trim, and paintings of flowers brighten the walls.

In the main lobby were paintings and plaques of Mary Horton, the founder, and of other early dignitaries. Along the left hallway were archival photographs of nurses, wards and brass plaques, concerning people that had donated much to the hospital. The Horton has Yolanda to thank for this impressive display; she dug them out of the archives, where they were just gathering dust. The telephone operator's office is still empty, and there isn't the bustle of the hospital I knew. But that is because just about all of the old hospital is offices. Although in these offices, one can still see the basic old wards; B-Ward now has medical secretaries, and it still has its ghost; the only difference is, that now that it no longer has all the bustle and noise during the day. They also hear the door open, and the footsteps during the day, and no one will work there late, we had no choice! Where supply was, is now the cashier's offices and accounting. Holbech Ward is now the Day Unit, the layout is very similar. Sister's office is gone; that is now in one of the end rooms previously used for sick children needing isolation. The back rooms, where the babies with spina bifida and hydrocephalus stayed, has been changed the most, to what now looks like speciality rooms. The whole unit is now accessed from the back, through a new hallway.

Outpatients and the plaster room, that was attached to emergency room, is the same, except the connecting door to the old ER is closed off. The old emergency rooms are now part of the outpatients.

At the other end, past the main entrance, is X-ray. That is now the personnel offices. They stay cool all the time, because the lead lined walls still exist. What was Norris Ward, is now a very large exercise room for out and inpatients.

Probably the biggest and most impressive change, is the old hospital kitchen. It used to be infested with cockroaches; now the area has offices and classrooms for the education department. Across the hall from that are the administrative offices, and the board room.

The Chapel/morgue has been changed to occupational health – the creaking yew trees have gone. The exit door, from the old main corridor to the occupational health, still exists. The exterior of the nurses' home looks much the same. What was the new dining room is still there- I'm not sure what that is now; possibly social services. My bedroom window, that was a thoroughfare for the nurses to come in after curfew, would no longer be a good access; outside the window the terrain is a bank that slopes quite steeply down, and it is in full view of the new part of the hospital.

On my second trip to the Horton, Yolanda and I toured the new part, while Mike took pictures of some of the archival photos and information. The new part is huge, and yet it still had the good feeling of the old smaller hospital of my day. The people were friendly and helpful. The hospital now has 250 beds; the medical beds are in a separate building from the surgical beds. The overall theme of decoration, in the Medical building, is beige/pale pink walls, with a burgundy trim. The orthopaedic and surgical units, although separate from one another, but because its building is attached to the old part, it continues with the pale blue and royal blue trim. There was obviously excellent planning as to where different services were placed. Physiotherapy is central to the departments that would use it the most. Occupational Therapy is close to Rowan Day Hospital (Where patients that live in their own homes, come to Rowan Day Hospital for the day, to receive therapy and counselling/teaching).

In the centre of the hospital, is a beautiful new chapel, which is not at all spooky! The hospital dining room is now called the restaurant, as it should because that is what it looks like. The only downside is, that temporarily, it is closing after 3:00 pm. I have always maintained that if people, especially a large number of people, are required to cover 24 hours a day, then food and drinks should be available to them during the traditional 'off hours', and not just via vending machines. The plan is for it to be open for all shifts. Even if it is only manned by a skeleton crew, and only a limited menu is available, it will be better. At least the wards have their own kitchens, where I am sure the evening and night staff can prepare food for themselves.

The operating theatre suite now has 4 theatre rooms, I was only allowed in the general entrance area – that is as it should be. The A&E has easy access for both walking and ambulance patients, with the ambulance patients not having to go through the general waiting area. There were several examining areas very busy, but, from what I could see, well equipped, and with adequate space to work. The waiting room was pleasant, and looked like they had comfortable chairs.

There is a separate Horton Treatment Care Unit, for the prevention of surgical/orthopaedic cases from backing up.

There is also a postgraduate building with a library in it, for the house doctors and the Horton physicians and surgeons. Obstetrics is still housed in the separate building, that was built just before I left in 1962. It has been extensively updated, and even has a birthing pool, for the mothers that want that method of delivery.

I have saved the best for last, and this really shows the commitment that the local people still have towards the Horton. Paediatrics ward. In 2001, the NHS paid for the construction of the building, it is at garden level so that there is an outside secure play area. It is very well planned, with all the rooms having windows, and treatment areas being centrally located. All necessary sinks etc are at child's height. The older children are separate from the younger ones, and have computers available for games at each bed. What I especially like was that these rooms were long and narrow, but wide enough to work, and space for added medical equipment. This way each bed was beside the window, and the children were facing each other, much more conducive for communicating, and yet easily made private. There were fun type decorations everywhere. In the treatment room, there were large Disney characters painted on the walls. These were done, at no charge, by a local artist. After the building was finished, the unit was going to need equipment, and

Christmas decorations Children's Ward 2006

furnishings - the works. There was no budget for it. The money was raised by the local people of Banburyshire, to the amount of over £360,000. In today's money probably well over £500,000. There was one local donor who contributed £65,000, but the rest was from all the local business people, and residents. When area people put that much time and money, into what they consider their hospital, it shows how committed and dedicated they are. To even consider closing it, is like a slap in their faces.

I believe, if the NHS was to give the hospital staff and the local people, a chance to work out a viable solution to the current budget problems, they would probably be surprised at what could be accomplished. Once things or places are closed, it is very hard to re-open them. It is a bit like closing the barn door after the horse is gone.